KEEPING IN TOUCH

Dedication

Sr Mary Reidy
(Daughter of Jesus)

for so many years of devoted care

Inigo Texts Series: 10

KEEPING IN TOUCH

POSTHUMOUS PAPERS ON IGNATIAN TOPICS

INCLUDING TRIBUTES BY VARIOUS AUTHORS

Michael Ivens, SJ

Edited by
Joseph A. Munitiz, SJ

GRACEWING

First published in 2007

Gracewing		Inigo Enterprises
2 Southern Avenue		Links View
Leominster	and	Traps Lane, New Malden
Herefordshire HR6 0QF		Surrey KT3 4RY

'The expense is recknoned; the enterprise is begun
It is of God . . .'

ISBN 978 0 85244 145 9

Typesetting by
Action Publishing Technology Ltd, Gloucester, GL1 5SR

CONTENTS

Contents

INTRODUCTION

Michael Ivens had been working on a 'glossary' – provisionally entitled *Ignatian Words* – even while completing his commentary on the *Spiritual Exercises* of St Ignatius of Loyola.[1] The first plan was to include the glossary in the commentary, but he was persuaded to make a second volume of it, partly in the hope that this would hasten publication of the first volume (as Michael was notorious for endless re-writing and correction of his texts).

On his death several versions of the different entries proposed for the glossary were found in his computer files and his print-outs, but all had in common that they followed an alphabetical sequence: some of these had been marked by him as 'done', more as 'nearly complete', a few were 'in progress', and others 'waiting to be done' (see the Table below). There were some tantalizing glimpses of themes (e.g. 'Etc.'), but also some serious absences (e.g. Discernment, but see the entry on Consolation/Desolation). Among the papers there were occasional notes on themes not mentioned in the lists (e.g. 'Kingdom', 'Liberality', 'Principle and Foundation', 'See', 'Seek and Find', 'Tempter', 'Two Standards', 'Use', and 'World'), but all were fragmentary. It was clear that the original project was far from complete, and there were even doubts if anything of real

---

[1] *Understanding the Spiritual Exercises: Text and Commentary: A Handbook for Retreat Directors*, published by Gracewing and Inigo Enterprises, Leominster 1998.

worth could be salvaged from such disparate materials.[2]

Fortunately it soon became apparent that there was an organic relationship linking many of the entries. Gradually a pattern emerged. So although readers should feel free to dip into these papers as the spirit moves them, they will not be defrauded if they follow the sequence in which they appear. The broad categories are:

1 terms that relate to what may be called the theological infrastructure;
2 terms that belong more specifically to the structure of the *Exercises*;
3 terms that explore the world of feelings that grow out of the experience of the *Exercises*.

Quite frequently these themes overlap, and a certain amount of repetition was inevitable; clearly there are certain convictions and principles dear to Michael's heart – marked by his breadth, tolerance, respect and firmness.

Among the papers there were also some typescripts of talks, and even possible drafts of chapters for the book he had intended to write on Ignatius (even signing a contract to this effect with Darton, Longman & Todd). However, all this material had become dated, and Michael showed no interest in their publication, nor indeed in the republication of the many articles he had contributed to *The Way* and *The Way Supplement*. He felt that whatever of value he still had to say would be included in the glossary, and for this reason the present publication is limited to that material.

At the end of this book, a number of items are added that fill out the portrait of this gifted interpreter and very brave man. The whole is dedicated with affection to the sister,

---

[2] An additional factor that may have slowed the project was the realization that the Spanish Jesuits were producing a very full glossary of Ignatian words; they invited Michael to contribute to this, and he did send a list of terms, but ill-health prevented any further work. He was not aware of the project undertaken by Willi Lambert, S.J., at about this time: cf. *Aus Liebe zur Wirklichkeit. Grudndworte ignatianischer Spiritualität*, Mainz, 2005.

Mary Reidy, who kept him alert, and as healthy as was possible in his final years. The illustration (p. 81), drawn by Michael, comes from one of several Christmas cards designed by him. His early interest in painting is mentioned in the Funeral homily by Gerard W. Hughes. Finally, the Editor gratefully acknowledges the help given at the proof-correction stage by both Mrs Jo Whale and Mrs Oonagh Walker.

List of Proposed 'Ignatian Words' – and stage of preparation as indicated in lists drawn up by Michael Ivens
(* asterisks = inclusion in this volume;
Italics = a non-Ignatian word;
[ ] square brackets = no corresponding text has been found among the papers)

'DONE' *Abhorrence, *Affection, *Agendo contra, *Colloquy, *Confusion, *Enemy, *Examen, *Fear, *Glory, *History, *Holy Spirit, *Humility, *Illuminism, *Indifference, *Intention, *Interior/Inner, *Love, *Marriage, *Reverence

'NEARLY COMPLETE' *Atonement Theology, *Contempt, *Creation, *Desire, *Devotion, *Divine titles, *Election, *Guigo, *Graces, *Imagination, *Imitation, *Mary, Mediation (see *Mary), *Paschal mystery, *Perfection (included in *State of Life), *Petition, *Poverty, *Powers of the soul, *Profit, *Religious Life, *Repose day, Seek and find, *Service, *Soul, *State of Life, *Trinity, *Vainglory, *Vocation, *Will of God

'IN PROGRESS' *Abnegation, Above, All Things cf. *God in all things, *Apophatic Theology, cf. *Mysticism, *Prayer. *Pride, *Riches

'TO BE DONE' *Apostolate, [Benefice], *Body, Christ, Cisneros, Consider, Contemplation, [Conversion], Covetousness, Counsels, Desolation, Discernment, Etc., Exercise, Honour, King, Knowledge, *Lectio divina, Liberality, [Ludolph of Saxony], Materia subjecta, Meditation, Mendicancy, *Mortal Sin, Mercy, Method of *prayer, [Movement of the *soul], Road, [Separation], [Shame], [Sin], [Union]

ABBREVIATIONS

* an asterisk next to a term indicates that the term has an entry in this volume.

[ ] square brackets around notes are used to indicate those added by the Editor.

CIS	Centrum Ignatianum Spiritualitatis
Constitutions	*The Constitutions of the Society of Jesus,* translated with an Introduction and a Commentary by George E. Ganss, Institute of Jesuit Sources, St Louis 1970
Contemplatio	'The Contemplation to Attain Love' [Exx. 230–237]
de Guibert	Cf. Bibliography
Directories	Palmer, Martin E., *On Giving the Spiritual Exercises.*
Exercises/Exercises	in italics to refer to the text, otherwise to the practice.
[Exx.]	*The Spiritual Exercises* (with the number of the paragraph)
General Examen of Candidates	Preliminary text to the *Constitutions*
MHSI	Monumenta Historica Societatis Iesu
Personal Writings	See Works of St Ignatius, Translation
Understanding	Ivens, Michael, *Understanding the Spiritual Exercises*, Gracewing, Leominster 1998.

Part I
Theological Themes

All things in God and God in all things

How is one to understand Ignatius' position on commitment to immediate realities, realities other than God, i.e. persons (for whom the word *love is properly used) but also study, ministry, office etc. Ignatius moves around this area freely and I shall do the same.

The general position is clear: there is a situation which Ignatius does not seem to regard as an altogether rare grace in which the two loves come together in harmony, so that in our relationship with creatures we find God, and in our relationship with the Creator God we find God's own loved creatures. He describes it in various ways. Twice in the *Exercises* he speaks about a love that is somehow sensed as descending from above, and in which God shines forth:

> The love that moves me has to descend from above ... so that the person who makes the choice must feel interiorly that the love felt for the object chosen is solely for the sake of one's Creator and Lord;[1]

and

> The love that moves me ... should descend from above ... so I must first of all feel within myself that the love, greater or lesser, that I have for these people is for God, and that in my motive for loving them more, God must shine forth.[2]

But in the world we know, and given the complexities and ambiguities within ourselves, this is obviously not going to be quite as simple as it might sound, and when we look a bit more closely at Ignatius' language we see that he attaches some highly demanding conditions. Thus, authentic love requires right *intention and a liberation from disordered *affections. More specifically, in some sense it excludes love of the creature 'for itself' and requires that in some sense love be taken from the creature and transferred to the Creator. Especially challenging at first sight, is the use in two texts of

---

[1] Second Way in the Third Time of Election [Exx. 184].
[2] First of the Rules for Almsgiving [Exx. 338].

the word 'only'. The problem is not that those terms make us aware that the synthesis of loves is demanding, but that they can seem to imply that it is less than it seems to be: does it leave any room for an appreciation of creatures in themselves, or does it, in fact, involve a certain diminution of our immediate loves and commitments, a toning down of their human fullness? In the case of each of these texts misreadings must be avoided, but without trivializing the Ignatian synthesis by underrating its real demands.

Here, as in many other contexts, note that Ignatius' preoccupation with transcending disordered *affection can give the impression that the antithesis of a disordered affection is no affection at all, affective neutrality. In fact the consequence of moving beyond disordered affection is not the affective void but a life of 'ordered' or converted affectivity. Basically, one can only relate authentically to a creature by allowing it to be a creature, and the essence of creaturehood is the creature's relationship with its creator and Lord. There is a sense, moreover, in which loving a creature 'for itself' means, in fact, not so much loving it for itself as for one's own self. In the case of non-human loves e.g. love of *riches and honour, this is obvious, but it can apply no less to human loves, though one should avoid facile disparagement of every kind of 'need love'. More practically, these at first sight uncomfortable terms recall that growth in integrity is not without its discontinuities, moments in which the demands of integrity might *not* feel like a relinquishment of something good.

This brings us to the 'only' of the *General Examen* at the start of the *Constitutions*.[3] This must be interpreted in the

---

[3] 'Everyone who enters the Society, following the counsel of Christ our Lord that *He who leaves father*, etc. [Matthew 19:29; Luke 18:30], should judge that he should leave his father, etc. ... Consequently he should endeavour to put aside all merely natural affection for his relatives and convert it into spiritual, by loving them **only** with that love which rightly ordered charity requires. He should be as one who is dead to the world and to self-love and who lives only for Christ our Lord, while having Him in place of parents, brothers, and all things', *General Examen of Candidates*, ch. 4, §7 (tr., Ganss, p. 95).

light of another principle of Ignatian exegesis: that in the
Exercises and *Constitutions* the general significance of a text
must be read in relation to the part of the process/sequence in
which it occurs. Here the section is concerned with explana-
tions given to candidates, who are being told the attitude that
will be especially important for novices in whom the essential break with the bonds of family may not be complete.
Nevertheless, today we might wish to find more in Ignatius
on the actual experience of integrated love and commitment.
Fortunately there are many indications in his life that love in
God does not lose the natural human qualities, but conse-
crates them. There is the witness of his friendships, the
quality of his relationships. In both the *Exercises* and the
Constitutions many texts leave us in no doubt that love and
commitment mean what we expect them to mean. The
Kingdom [Exx. 91] is about the consecration of all one's
resources, including ambition, that a generous male of the
time might bring to a crusade.

The pre-occupation with God as Creator and Lord affects
the way Ignatius experiences all reality; 'all things' (*todas
las cosas*) – an expression that brings out the range and
complexity of immediate reality – are not just God's
creation; they are His creatures.

Creatures are referred to in a number of places by the
word 'things', which designates them not in relation to God
but in their immediate relationship to ourselves, as objects
of sense, and feeling, as material of use and choice. The
term 'all things' includes implicitly not only material
things, but situations and events, and the entire range of
finite reality in its range and complexity.

The use of the words 'things' and 'all things' recognizes
that immediate reality has its own meaning and consistency,
and that while all things are indeed created things, they do
not make us relate them to God, and do not automatically
lead to Him, but only insofar as we should wish them to,
and indeed take positive steps to counter the instincts that
keep a thing referred to ourselves. We relate to things
according to their own truth, however, when we 'find God

in them', and love them in a way completely integrated
with our love of their (and our) Creator and Lord.

Apostolate

In what sense can the spirituality of the *Exercises* be said
to be 'apostolic'? In some ways the answer is clear: the
Exercises provide

- (i)   the basis for a spirituality of finding God in all things,[4]
- (ii) a 'theology of the apostolate' in the elements of the
        Kingdom exercise [Exx. 91–98], and its extension into the
        Incarnation contemplation [Exx. 101–109]: God's entry in
        Christ into the 'real' world, Christ's mission to liberate
        that world from its enemies, the need for people to
        continue this mission through the course of history;
- (iii) involvement in Christ's mission, which is also involve-
        ment in his situation and style (*imitation): the particular
        way of life envisaged under the rubric of 'evangelical
        perfection' is that of the 'preacher in poverty';
- (iv) the directedness of the *Exercises* to *election; this is apos-
        tolic in more senses than one, as it puts before every
        exercitant the possibility that they are themselves called to
        the expressly apostolic life, but it is also a school for a
        spirituality of 'daily life', in which union is understood not
        as union of mind in contemplation, but as union of will in
        a continual discernment of the *will of God in the choices
        of life;
- (v)   apostolic awareness, even when made in radical separation
        from the world.

---

[4] Especially in the Principle and Foundation [Exx. 23] and in the *Contem-
     platio ad amorem* [Exx. 232–237].

However, even in their day, the *Exercises* did not, and still do not, deal with specific forms of apostolate. Note also that for all his highly developed sense of the distinctiveness of the apostolic vocation and spirituality, Ignatius does not press the distinction between spiritualities as far as we tend to do today – in the sense that he saw the *Exercises* as quite suitable for Carthusians (and indeed in his last letter, dated on the day of his death, he commends a Carthusian prior to accept a young man who has offered himself to the Society but was debarred by physical deformity[5]).

The milieu in which the *Exercises* came into existence and developed to their final textual form was the personal apostolic spirituality as lived first by Ignatius alone and then with companions in the years from his conversion to the foundation of the Society. In their early days the *Exercises* were given mainly, but not exclusively, to people whose spirituality was 'apostolic' in the above sense – Jesuits, other priests, laypeople in positions of influence, young people seeking a state of life, especially those willing to enter the Society, if called to do so. Drawing on today's clarities regarding the contemplative/apostolic distinction, we would say that they are used increasingly to nourish and stimulate men and women engaged in some way in the apostolate.

Certain questions therefore arise: in what sense do the *Exercises* further an apostolic spirituality? Should they be adapted to serve modern apostolic needs directly, or to promote apostolic insights that were still below the horizon at the time of Ignatius? If in principle use of the *Exercises* to promote the apostolate is a right use, are there nevertheless ways of using the *Exercises* that do not fit their nature and purpose?

It might be said that the *Exercises* are calculated to bring

---

[5] Letter to Leonard Kessel, Cologne, with a covering note to the Rectors of Jesuit houses where the man might stay *en route* there, MHSI *Epistolae* XII, Nos. 6739, 6740, pp. 199–200; the young Frenchman had something wrong with his eyes.

about a general sense of apostolic meaning, as a call to collaborate in Christ's work in the world on the basis of a relationship of 'imitation', which will express itself particularly in the values of the Two Standards. But the *Exercises* do not substitute for the experience that can only happen over longer periods of time than thirty days. They are not the natural situation in which to make a decision, or experience a change of outlook which would ordinarily suppose an experience not available in the course of the Twentieth Annotation retreat (the full thirty days 'enclosed' retreat), or gain familiarity with concepts or projects which would ordinarily be discovered in reading or personal contact.

Atonement Theology

Atonement theology attempts to give a systematic answer to the question: why the Cross? Why was it necessary (indeed was it necessary at all?) that our redemption be brought about by Christ's passion and death? There are various atonement theologies, and in connection with giving the *Exercises* it is well to be aware of two such theologies in particular, the 'satisfaction' theory of St Anselm, and the more recent 'penal substitution' theory.

The first is based on the model of reconciliation in feudal relationships; it sees human sin as a dishonour to God requiring satisfaction. This can be given only by a member of the human race, perpetrator of the offence, but because the dishonoured person is God, satisfaction can be given only by a human being who is himself God. According to the penal substitution theory, Christ in his passion and death took upon himself our punishment, thus appeasing the

Father's wrath. The first view, though never incorporated into official church doctrine and not today generally accepted, was widely held until recent times. The second arose in the Reformation and was the standard view in many evangelical churches. Despite *prima facie* resemblances, the two should not be confused

In the *Exercises* we find no attempt to 'explain' the passion. Ignatius simply sets out the basic revealed truths for the exercitant to contemplate, and to dwell on the thoughts that contemplation suggests: the Trinitarian decision that the Second Person should become human to save the human race [Exx. 102], the 'descent' of the Creator and his death in time on the Cross [Exx. 53], his extreme human suffering [Exx. 48, 195, 196, 203], and 'for my sins' [Exx. 53, 193]. The exercitant assimilates these truths by an imagination-aided contemplation, but is not tied to any particular 'theology of atonement'. From the very first meditation with its colloquy, 'imagining Christ our Lord present before me and nailed to the Cross' [Exx. 53], the essential position of the *Exercises* is clear: the exercitant is to 'ponder whatever comes to mind', conscious simply of the destructive mystery of sin and of the 'self-emptying' of Christ on the Cross 'for my sins', as God's gratuitous response. The implicit reference to Philippians 2:7 ('who emptied himself, taking the form of a slave') in the language of the colloquy (the descent of the Creator 'from eternal life to temporal death') is confirmed by the use in the Vulgate of the phrase *se exinanivit* (found in the Latin text of the Christological hymn).

Body

The exercitant is a body-person. As such, he or she seeks
and finds God and his will in and through responses of
choice, rejection or acceptance in relation to bodily situations, conditions and forms of bodily experience. Various
applications of this principle punctuate the *Exercises*.

At the outset, the exercitant learns to begin a period of
*prayer with a body ritual – a miniscule entry procession
and an act of *reverence [Exx. 75]; the exercitant must then
adopt the bodily position or positions that help one to find
or sustain a sought *grace [Exx. 76]. In dealing with the
body in prayer, it is only when he comes to the subject of
posture that Ignatius makes no specific recommendation,
leaving decision to the exercitant. It is noticeable, certainly,
that the positions he mentions are all those of bodily still-
ness; for Ignatius walking was for reflection rather than for
contemplation or meditation. But with this proviso it can be
said that for Ignatius the position of the body in prayer,
precisely   because   important,   cannot   be   generally
prescribed, but must be a matter of the individual's sense
of the effects of the spirit-body link at a particular moment.

As an ambience for meditation on sin, Ignatius proposes
an environment of bodily darkness. Experiences of bodily
discomfort give authenticity and commitment to the dispositions and desires that are the bases of penance. The
natural pleasures of the seasons can be used to enhance
contemplation of the Resurrection [Exx. 229]. In the Third
Way of Praying [Exx. 258] the bodily function of breath-
ing is enlisted as an aid to contemplation.

In order to appreciate – and apply in a particular case –
Ignatius' directives on the body in prayer, the director must
keep two points in mind. First, a literal or fundamentalist
attitude towards these would be contrary to the *Exercises*
themselves. The recommendations regarding darkness are
in an Addition (nr. 7 [Exx. 79]) and Ignatius' application
of the Additions is flexible. Forms and frequency of
penance are discovered in the end by personal discernment

and judgement (cf. Addition 10, especially [Exx. 89]).
However, neither in the *Exercises*, nor elsewhere in his
writings can Ignatius be said to be soft on the body. Characteristic of his attitude is a concern to find the mean
between demanding too much of the body and asking too
little. This concern, rooted in extravagances following his
own conversion, could be illustrated in detail from both the
correspondence and the *Constitutions*. In the *Exercises*, it
appears in the insistence that decisions in the matter of
penance be personal and based on experiment.

Creation

In the *Exercises* Creator and Creation belong to the positive vision of creation established at the outset in the Principle and Foundation [Exx. 23]. But first, a caveat: it is
easy gravely to distort Ignatius by facile presentations of
his 'positive outlook on creation', such as any presentation
which plays down (i) Ignatius' consciousness of the sin of
the world or in ourselves, or (ii) his insistence that a
mature Christian, whatever form of life one may be called
to lead, desires in some sense – if only in the sense of
setting a value upon – the paradoxes of Christ's way (as
presented in the Two Standards and the Third Mode of
Humility). The actual forms of a person's relationship to
immediate material or social realities will depend on situations and circumstances, and also on choices discerned in
the spirit; but there must be what might be termed the 'attitudinal frame' within which these elements of Ignatian
spirituality are discerned. A complete study of this
outlook, which Ignatius himself never systematized, would

need to draw on the entire range of his writings, and in particular on his own account of insights gained at the end of his sojourn at Manresa, which he associates particularly with the illumination on the banks of the river Cardoner and the visions preceding it. The essential are to be found however in the creation vocabulary of the *Exercises* and his ways of using it.

When Ignatius designates God as Creator and Lord of the material realities and the events and situations which make the category of 'all things', he is saying something more for these than that God created, willed or at least providentially permitted them. He is making a claim about God's here and now presence and action, and also about the ultimate purpose of *all things. Thus as creator of all things and as Lord of all that happens within his creation God is in countless ways involved in our reality, in and through 'all things' working for us, caring for us, reaching out to us and revealing himself. Moreover, God's action in the world for us corresponds to the purpose for which the world exists and the ultimate reason why under God the things happen that do. All that exists and happens, in the way of events and situations, is created, willed or permitted by God for one end only: to help human beings to attain God's purpose for individuals and the human race – namely, salvation, through praise, worship, and *service of God.

We respond to these fundamental truths about reality at two interrelated levels: that of the 'ordered use' prescribed in the Principle and Foundation, and that of the insight and experience, which are the grace of the *Contemplatio*. For a spirituality of 'all things' both levels are essential. The level of 'ordered use' is essential; for what differentiates the human being from all other creatures is that our place in the world, the ways we fit into it, are not pre-determined, but we deal with our material environment, and respond to events and situations, through free and purposive choices (which include choices of inaction, avoidance or repudiation). And it is precisely on this basis – as users of reality – that we are able to live in the world salvifically, by choices of use and avoidance ordered to the praise, reverence, and service of God.

Ordered use, then, is essential, but to remain there would be a seriously incomplete picture of Ignatian spirituality as a way of responding to God in and through all things, as prescribed in the Foundation. Through choices by which we establish ourselves in a right relationship with immediate reality the way is opened to another and more contemplative way in which our faith-relationship with God develops through all things: viz. the level at which in all things we find a God who 'uses' all things to give himself to us. As we 'find' God in this way we begin to experience the world as the *milieu divin*[6] transparent to God's presence within it for us, to sense the goodness of God in everything in a way that makes everything a support and a stimulus for the complete gift of self expressed in the *Sume et suscipe*, 'Take Lord and receive' [Exx. 234].

Though separated by the length of the Four Weeks, the two texts, the Foundation and the *Contemplatio* represent complementary processes of a unified spirituality. Only a person who is seeking God in the right patterns of use and avoidance is open to an authentic experience of reality in the mode of the *Contemplatio*. But the more one grows in the spirituality of the *Contemplatio*, really experiencing the whole world as the divine context, the more one is motivated to discern the uses of reality that make for praise reverence and service (cf. [Exx 39]). Without the never outgrown *discipline* inculcated by the Foundation, a spiritual outlook claiming to be based on the *Contemplatio* could become shallow and even illusory. Without the experience of the *Contemplatio,* a spirituality based on the Foundation alone could be voluntaristic and arid; and would lack precisely that transforming vision of God in all things that is the key to Ignatius' apostolic versatility and audacity.

This summary may not leave a modern reader wholly satisfied, but the main lines of the theology of creation

---

6   [The title of Teilhard de Chardin's celebrated work.]

undergirding the *Exercises* may suffice to illustrate the theological outlook that gives Ignatian spirituality its freedom and flexibility.

The Cross

In the *Exercises* the Cross is the object of the exercitant's attention not only in the Third Week; it is central also to the First Week, where the opening exercise culminates in a contemplation of the Cross [Exx. 53]. This will remain in the memory to provide the implicit context of the following meditation with its colloquy of mercy, and to which the exercitant will return in the repetition. The place of the Cross in the First Week tends to be missed by those who fail to appreciate the importance in the *Exercises* of colloquy and repetitions. Further indications of the significance of the Cross in the *Exercises* are the emphasis on glory *through* suffering and labour: cf. the Call of the earthly king [Exx. 93] and the Second Week triple colloquies [Exx. 147].

Contemplation of the Cross, as the text of the *Exercises* acknowledges, is a deeply personal matter. In the first meditation, for instance, the exercitant is told to 'go over whatever comes to mind' [Exx. 53]. Nevertheless, certain principles are set out. The Cross is significant because through it the exercitant is personally saved: on the Cross Christ suffered and died 'for me' and 'for my sins'. To this the exercitant's response is one of shame, confusion, and grief, leading to deep contrition, compassion, and a renewed commitment to serve Christ and suffer for him.

The intensely personal contemplation of Christ during

the *Exercises* carries over into the exercitant's subsequent life as an ongoing participation in the pattern of Christ's death and resurrection, in and through inner experience, activity, events and situations (the Paschal mystery). It is lived out particularly in the *poverty and humility exemplified in the Cross as Christ's final self-emptying [Exx. 53]; in labouring and suffering with Christ in the apostolate [Exx. 95]; in the extension of compassion to other people, Christ's members.

It is instructive to note that in the 'experiments'[7] of the Jesuit novitiate the making of the 'Spiritual Exercises' is followed by the experience of living and working in a hospital – for Ignatius that was the Third Week in action. The same attitude underlies the provision in the *Constitutions* that a person wishing to return to the Society after leaving it should be placed for a time in a hospital to serve Christ's poor 'for His love'.[8]

Divine titles

The word 'God', without qualification, is used in the *Exercises* mainly in connection with statements of truth or of principle.[9] But running through the *Exercises* a variety of divine titles express aspects of our relationship with a personal God who is our 'Lord', 'Creator and Redeemer',

---

7 The *Constitutions* recommend that novices should undergo a series of *experiencias* ('tests'), hence the traditional term 'experiments': *General Examen of Candidates,* ch. 4, §64–70 (tr., Ganss, pp. 95–8). §§64–70.
8 *Constitutions* Part II, c. 4, §6D [288] (Ganss, p. 151).
9 For example [Exx. 58, 59, 150, 154, 184].

'Divine Majesty', 'Goodness', 'Divine Justice', and so on.
Most of the titles are attributed at times to the Three
Persons, at times specifically to Christ. Sometimes the attribution is clear from the context; in particular cases, there
can be room for different opinions on the right attribution
(as in the case of the titles used in the Contemplation to
attain Love[10]).

In general it may be said that in the application of titles
one should acknowledge both the Trinitarian and Christo-
centric dimensions of the *Exercises*. God our 'Lord'
frequently – some would say usually – refers to Christ.[11]
While in many cases the sense of the titles needs no explanation, a note on three of them may be in place.

1. *God our Lord*: a title blending elements of *reverence,
   familiarity and *affection. It occurs with so much
   frequency in the *Exercises* that it might be described as
   Ignatius' ordinary way of conceiving of God. Its main
   context is that of *service, but it is also prominent in the
   context of *prayer e.g. 'to ask God our Lord ...' [Exx. 16,
   48, etc.], 'I will conclude with a colloquy ... conversing
   with God our Lord' [Exx. 61], 'I will ... consider how
   God our Lord ['my Lord Jesus' in the Vulgate] is looking
   at me' [Exx. 75].
2. *Divine Majesty*: a title used both of Christ (e.g. [Exx. 146])
   and of the Trinity (e.g. [Exx. 106]). Its context is never
   casual, but always that of highly motivated self-offering.[12]
3. *Divine Goodness*: the Spanish term *bondad* carries the
   overtone of kindness.

---

[10] See *Understanding*, p. 172, n. 19.
[11] For example [Exx. 38, 39, 135, 138, 155, 343]. However, Christ is
      also *Creator* [Exx. 53], *Eternal Lord* [Exx. 63, 65, 98], *Creator and
      Lord* [Exx. 16], *Eternal King* [Exx. 95], *Universal Lord* [Exx. 97],
      Eternal Lord of All Things [Exx. 98], *Infinite Goodness* [Exx. 98], *Holy
      Majesty* [Exx. 98], *Divine Majesty* [Exx. 146–147], *Consoler* [Exx.
      224].
[12] Cf. Annotations 5, 16, 20 [Exx. 5, 16, 20]; the preparatory prayer
      [Exx. 46]; the definition of the Third Class [Exx. 155], and of the Third
      Kind of Humility [Exx. 167]; also in connection with Election [Exx.
      183].

Glory of God

Reference to the 'glory of God', with the distinctive qualification of 'greater' is one of the salient characteristics of
Ignatian spirituality.[13] A modern reader would be seriously
mistaken in playing down its importance on the grounds
that the concept of 'glory' would have appealed naturally to
a person of his background. The central motif of Ignatian
spirituality is not a reflection of obsolete cultural values,
but, while characterized by certain distinctive emphases,
has its roots in scripture and tradition.

Glory and 'giving glory'

In Scripture the word 'glory' (*kābôd*) as applied to God,
designates the very being of God, the 'godness' of God. In
the eschatalogical kingdom the vision of this glory will be
our joy and the satisfaction of our deepest yearnings. The
glory of God also extends into God's entire creative and
redemptive presence and action in the world. There,
however, it is not yet manifest in its ultimate radiance and
beauty; often it is embedded in obscure and paradoxical
forms – even that of crucifixion. It is present in a particular way wherever the processes of God come about through
human freedom, acting with the intention that God be God
in a human life, in human society and in the world.

We 'give' glory when we contemplate or praise God's
glory, but we do so also through the quality of our lives and
especially through the actions and decisions of *service.

---

[13] [In his notes Ivens acknowledges his debt to the article, 'Gloire ('La
plus grande gloire de Dieu')', by François Courel, *Dictionnaire de
Spiritualité*, t. VI, Paris 1967, cols. 487–94; in particular (col. 491),
with regard to the service of God and the service of others, 'It is the
mysticism of the pursuit of the glory of God that brings the two into
unity; through it the service of our neighbours leads us to the service
of God, and the same movement of the service of God brings us back
ceaselessly to the love of neighbour. The two phases of the action are
linked into a single action: we are at the service of the glory of God
(*nous sommes au service de la gloire de Dieu*).' Fr Courel taught him
in Lyon (see Biography and Publications).]

The contemplation and praise of the glory of God in everything is of course a constant and fundamental stance in the *Exercises*. In the text, aspects of the glory of God in the world (not always designated by the word itself) are proposed for contemplation in the Second Meditation of the First Week [Exx. 59–60], in the Kingdom exercise [Exx. 95], in the Incarnation contemplation [Exx. 102], and the *Contemplatio ad amorem* [Exx. 234–237]. In Ignatius' usage, however, both in the *Exercises* and elsewhere, the typical and normal context in which the term 'giving glory' occurs is other than that of formal contemplation. For giving glory to God, like loving God, consists not only, or even primarily, in words, but also in deeds – in the choices and actions by which we collaborate in the very processes by which God is glorified in the world. (e.g. [Exx. 16]). A particular characteristic of Ignatius' 'glory-language' brings out the connection between giving glory and *service, namely the fact that in the majority of cases where the formula 'give glory' appears, glory is proposed as the final criterion and control of decision [Exx. 180, 185]. Moreover, it is the connection between glory and service which accounts for the distinctive comparative: *greater* [Exx. 152, 240, 339]. This points to the greater quality of our service, reflecting the 'magis' of the Kingdom exercise [Exx. 98].

The practical implications of referring all choices to the criterion of the *greater glory* of God may not always be obvious. Desire for God's glory will not in every case be enough to remove uncertainties or bypass the need for discernment and other elements of the decision-making process. It could be said, indeed, that the main effect of Ignatius' insistence on the glory of God is that it leads us to become 'glory conscious'. What glory consciousness does is to provide a general spiritual attitude, a faith-outlook within which all decision-making processes are undertaken.

While glory consciousness is permeated by the sense of the 'above', of divine transcendence, it does not devalue immediate reality. On the contrary, because he is always

conscious of the glory of God, Ignatius can experience the
world as a 'divine milieu' where God is found in '*all
things', even in the cramped and trivial realm of the worka-
day. Thus the glory of God invests with dignity and
meaning, without depriving the ordinary of its ordinariness
or distracting from its particular disciplines. In the *Constitutions*, as though to stress the point, Ignatius will appeal
to the glory of God as the criterion for decisions regarding
the quality of Jesuit clothes, whether a Jesuit should travel
on foot or horseback, with or without money.

Glory consciousness also helps the mind to focus on ultimate reality, to clarify essentials and bring freedom from
inessentials or unwarranted assumptions. Where everything
is considered in the light of the glory of God, false
absolutes are easily explored; when the glory of God is the
absolute, false absolutes are easily relativized.

Glory consciousness also affects some of the classic
tensions of Christian life. It helps us bring seemingly antithetical values into living synthesis by referring both to a
single ultimate reference. Thus it touches the tension we
experience between commitment to personal holiness and
commitment to building the kingdom of God in the world.
Because a glory conscious person desires that God be ever
more effectively God in our lives, glory consciousness
commits us totally to the quest for personal holiness with
its non-negotiable personal tasks. Because we desire totally
that God be God in the spread of his kingdom, so we live
and act that God be increasingly God in his world. We are
committed to participation in the processes that make for
God's glory, to discern his call to *service with a certain
self-forgetfulness, an 'altruism' towards God that leaves no
room for self-preoccupied or inappropriately private
approaches to personal holiness. In this connection it has
been observed that in the thought of Ignatius, his new religious order, unlike other orders of active life, did not have
a double end – personal perfection and the apostolate – but
that he saw both as synthesized into a single end, the glory
of God.

So we give glory to God when we respond to reality, especially when we make a choice, coming out of a certain intention and based on a certain conviction. The intention is so to respond to this here-and-now situation, even if it is ugly, unwanted or evil, in such a way that in my response God may be God, his will be done and his purposes fulfilled. The conviction is that since in everything the processes of the redeeming Christ are going on, then in no situation is it impossible to find the response, make the decision, that collaborates in the process of God's glory.

The glory of God may indeed be the consideration that most effectively reveals deep faith-meaning in painful, constrictive or positively evil situations, even in situations which result from our sinfulness or folly. For God is greater than any situation that tends of its nature to constrict, diminish, or even to leave us feeling trapped in sin. In everything the processes of the redeeming Christ are going on. It is therefore possible to respond to any situation in such a way that through our response God is God, even if with a glory for moments partly hidden.

Giving glory to God, like *love, is not a formality but a commitment, a way of being in relationship to God with consequences for the way a person experiences and responds to all reality. As such, it has in Ignatius a partic- ular emphasis and tone which comes from the connection of glory with two other themes of his spirituality: a strong sense of *creation and incarnation; and the inseparable connection between praise and *reverence on the one hand and *service on the other. But this does not mean that for the believer all is bathed in divine radiance. Where the glory of Christ's ongoing redemptive action is in combat to the death with the enemies of the kingdom, his glory even in the experience of faith is deeply obscure 'praise and service'. The more the world is perceived in faith, the more it can be experienced as a divine milieu, as – in Hopkins' phrase – 'charged with the grandeur of God'.

In general, it might be said that 'glory' for Ignatius brings together on the one hand his profound sense of divin-

ity – of the otherness which calls forth constant wonder and
reverential praise – and on the other his sense of God in the
world and of the service of the kingdom. To *desire God's
glory as the norm of one's action is to desire God's will,
but under the aspect of desiring to be involved in God's
action in his world – so to act that through one's response
God may be God.

Holy Spirit

Crucial to the effectiveness of the *Exercises* is the action of
the Holy Spirit in the exercitant. Yet the full title 'Holy
Spirit' is found only in five places, and always with direct
reference to a gospel text [the section entitled 'New Testament Materials for Contemplation'] and in a sense
'incidentally'.[14] In addition to these references, the phrase
'Spirit and Lord' [Exx. 365] is obviously used once as a
title for the Holy Spirit. But no other explicit references to
the Spirit are to be found in the *Exercises*, a fact which has
frequently contributed to misunderstandings of their nature.

One explanation has to do with the anti-Illuminist climate
in the Church, which imposed on Ignatius a need to be
careful to avoid incurring suspicion. 'Illuminism' is the
name given to a recurring movement in the history of spirituality characterized by claims to direct enlightenment
from the Holy Spirit establishing independence from objective authority (Church, Scripture, etc.). The presence of
illuminists (*alumbrados*) in Spain in the time of Ignatius,
resulting in a climate of suspicion towards new or charis-

---

14   [Exx. 263, 273, 304, 307, 312].

matic spiritual developments, had effects on Ignatius' own
history and on that of the *Exercises*. Even in the final years
of his life Ignatius had to contend with critics of the *Exercises* who claimed to find an illuminist flavour in them.
Prominent names among these were Silíceo (Archbishop of
Toledo), and the theologian, Melchor Cano, OP. In 1553
the Archbishop, backed by Cano, established a commission
to examine the *Exercises* under Tomás de Pedroche.
Although the *Exercises* had already been approved by Paul
III in 1548, Pedroche found parts of them heretical,
proclaiming in particular that the claim in Annotation 15
(that the Creator deals directly with the creature and the
creature with its Creator and Lord [Exx. 15]) is 'a statement made by an illuminist'. Silíceo did not press the
verdict. Nadal, however, answered Pedroche with an
Apologia for the *Exercises*.[15] In view of subsequent history,
the fact that the *Exercises* could have been originally seen
as containing free-spirit attitudes highlights the difference
between the *Exercises* themselves and ways in which they
were later interpreted and given.

But more important, it must be realized that the paucity
of explicit references, far from indicating a neglect of the
Spirit in the *Exercises* corresponds to the precise way in
which the Spirit is present in them: the Spirit is not the
object of *prayer (nowhere in the *Exercises* is the exercitant directed to make a prayer to the Spirit), rather the
effects of the Spirit and its felt presence are the *milieu* in
which prayer takes place. Hence there is *implicit* reference
to the Spirit wherever there is reference to the *action* of the
Spirit: in enlightenment [Exx. 2] and insight [Exx. 118], in
inner knowledge [Exx. 63], in the direct communication
between creature and creator [Exx. 15], in consolation
[Exx. 316, 329, 330], and all the effects ascribed to the
equivocally named 'good spirit' and 'good angel' [Exx.

---

[15] The long reply by Nadal is published in his correspondence: MHSI
Nadal: Epistolae 4, 820–73; the whole incident is described by Polanco
in his *Chronicon* MHSI 3, 335–36, with the text of the *censura* in an
Appendix, ibid., 503–24.

315, 335], in the entire range of the deep *affections given in response to *petition, in the instant clarity of the First Time of Election [Exx.175], the emerging *consolation of the Second [Exx. 176], the enlightenment of the intellect in the Third [Exx. 182], and in the *love that descends from above [Exx. 184, 338].

A director should be aware of this activity of the Spirit and help the exercitant to be aware of it: 'Now that the dangers and the exaggerations from Illuminism are scarcely present, the exercitant must be explicitly told that the Exercises will evoke, deepen, strengthen and make more explicit the ever-present experience of the Holy Spirit.'[16]

Imitation

To imitate Christ is in some sense to be Christ-like – in one's situation, way of behaving or, most importantly, in one's inner world of thoughts, feelings, attitudes and judgements. Basic to understanding the concept is the truth that we relate to Christ not just as a teacher or even as the exemplar of a way, but on the basis of a transforming union of life: 'it is no longer I who live, but Christ lives in me' (Galatians 2:20). Any authentic mode of imitation is therefore an expression and confirmation of this fundamental relationship.

In the *Exercises* imitation is the fruit of contemplating the person, words and actions of Christ in the episodes of the gospel story. Two modes of imitation in particular are specified as arising from this contemplation. First, one is led to

16 Harvey Egan, *Ignatian Mystical Horizon*, p. 122.

be Christ-like within the realm of the ordinary and everyday by imitating Christ in the use of the senses [Exx.
248], and especially in attitudes and conduct in regard to food
(notice in this connection the juxtaposition of the Rules for
Eating [Exx. 210–217] with the contemplation of the Last
Supper). However, imitation in the *Exercises* is associated
mainly with the themes of *poverty and of the experience
of contumely (cf. [Exx. 95, 139, 147, 167], to which must
be added the implicit reference to imitating Christ in
poverty [Exx. 344]). This latter form of imitation is closely
bound up in turn with the principle, basic to Ignatian spirituality, that Christ's mission, first entrusted to the
Apostles, is prolonged into history through the lives and
actions of successive generations of his servants and friends
[Exx. 146].

How far does imitation involve actual similarity with the
Jesus of the Gospels? At first sight the term might suggest
an ideal of imitating literally, in a sense mimicking, the
Christ presented in the Gospels (much as Ignatius at an
immature stage of development tried to mimic saintly
heroes). Such a concept, however, would be not only unrealistic but inimical to any authentically personal
life-in-Christ. Imitation does not eliminate the individuality
that makes one different from Jesus, or the uniqueness of
the ways in which every individual life witnesses to Christ
in cultures and situations other than those of first century
Palestine. The Person one imitates is a risen Person whose
presence in every individual is unique and personal ('for
Christ plays in ten thousand places, / Lovely in limbs, and
lovely in eyes not his'[17]). Perfection, then, requires the
form of imitation right for oneself; objective similarity to
the Christ of the Gospels is not its ultimate measure.

But if the link between imitation and the Gospels is not
one of literal mimicry, love-enlightened knowledge of the
Christ of the Gospels is nevertheless its norm. Moreover,
while there are many ways of imitation, some can be

---

[17]   Gerard Manley Hopkins, 'As kingfishers catch fire ...' (p. 51, no. 34).

described as being in a certain sense more 'literal' than others; and in the *Exercises* one prays for the grace to be more, rather than less, literally Christ-like in regard to the paradoxical pattern of life consisting in poverty with its multiple vulnerabilities. This pattern, indeed, is so fundamental that it must in some way be reflected in the lives of all who truly live 'in Christ'; but there are situations, transitory or lasting, characterized by a more literal resemblance to the situations of Christ's own life, situations in which in an obvious and immediate sense the disciple is like the master. Ignatius' position might be summed up by saying that commitment to the imitation of Christ implies on our side that we set a special value on such situations, while recognizing that the actual situations of our lives will depend on circumstances, providence, particular *vocation. Ignatius belongs to a tradition which holds that the imitation of Christ in poverty is particularly appropriate to the *apostolate, which he saw not only as doing the work of Christ, but doing it in the style of Christ.

Marriage

In the *Exercises* Ignatius seems to put marriage in the same category as priesthood [Exx. 172]. Both are unchangeable. Once entered upon, even if for questionable motives, there is no option but to lead a good life within them. Of both it is true that a choice made from disordered attachments is not a divine *vocation, and hence by implication in both states one can make a choice which *is* a divine vocation. In the case of *election of a way of life, a 'good election', i.e. one made solely for 'the service and praise of God our Lord

and the eternal salvation of my soul' [Exx. 169], marriage
is equated by Ignatius with a 'vocation' which is always
pure and clear and 'without disordered attachments' [Exx.
172].

On Ignatius' criteria for vocation the majority of people
could not claim to be in their 'states in life' on the basis of
a divine vocation. This does not mean that in every case
these people have made a disordered or bad choice, since
in many cases no personal choice was made at all. On this
point Ignatius could be said to exaggerate, and the reason
is obvious, namely his concern to establish the almost lost
concept of vocation. In the case of marriage, it could be
said that in today's world it can make more sense to speak
of marriage as a vocation in the strong sense, i.e. a situation freely chosen out of a *desire for God's service etc. In
the *Exercises* Ignatius is envisaging a person free to choose,
but matching the doctrine of the *Exercises* to the social
reality of Ignatius' time, is another question.[18]

---

[18] More information on Ignatius' attitude to marriage is available in Hugo
Rahner, *Saint Ignatius Loyola; Letters to Women*, Freiburg, Edinburgh-London, Herder, Nelson, 1960, cf. General Introduction and
Letters, pp. 17–18, 23–4; 138–45 (to Joanna Colonna), 215–16 (to
Margherita Gigli), 461–64 (to Isabel de Vega); his work for prosti-
tutes in Rome is well known, and his principle clearly was, 'The
unmarried women shall be quite free to marry or take the veil' (p.18);
but while generally accepting the common opinion of the age (that only
two alternatives were open to women: marriage or the veil), Ignatius
was prepared to allow an unmarried woman to remain as she was (p.
215); however, he also considered that so long as there was no question of obstructing a religious vocation, a person might marry out of
obedience (p. 461).

Mary

The *Exercises* contain Marian texts of various kinds. The *Hail Mary* (never to be perfunctorily 'brought in') is integral to the *prayer of the first two Weeks. The formulae offered as matter for contemplation in the Second and Third Ways of Prayer include the *Hail Holy Queen*. The self-offering of the Kingdom exercise is made with the witness and support of Mary as *Theotókos*, mother of the 'eternal Lord of all things'. Mainly, however, the Marian prayers of the *Exercises* fall into two categories: the contemplation of Mary in the Gospels [Exx. 101–126, 132, 134, 208, 218, 273, 276, together with 248], and the Triple Colloquies (cf. [Exx. 63]).

Contemplation of Mary in the Gospels opens the mind of the exercitant to many layers of meaning. It brings out Mary's integral association in the saving actions of Jesus; through it the exercitant comes to know the person of Mary; and known in this way Mary exemplifies the personal qualities sought in the *Exercises* themselves – docility to God's word, *poverty, humility, assimilation into Christ at every level, even in the 'use of the senses' [Exx. 248].

In the Triple Colloquies Mary is not so much an object of contemplation as an agent in the exercitant's present relationship with Christ and the Father, her role being to help the exercitant appreciate and desire the *graces which she then asks of her Son and Lord on their behalf. In the colloquies of the First Week, the exercitant turns to Mary in the awareness of her unique competence, founded in freedom from sin, to help him or her to find the insight into sin sought at this stage of the Exercises. In the Second Week, the *petitions will be made in the awareness, arising especially from the Infancy contemplations, of the ways in which Mary herself exemplifies the qualities petitioned.

Marian Titles

In the *Exercises*, Mary is referred to by name – outside the
Hail Mary – four times only, while 'Virgin', 'Virgin Mary'
and 'Handmaid of the Lord' appear once. The titles that
predominate are 'Mother' (thirteen times) and 'Our Lady'
(twenty-seven times).

As used of Mary, 'mother' has multiple associations.
First the word evokes mother and child imagery. This is
the focus of the opening contemplations of the Second
Week, and further indications of its place in Ignatius'
personal spirituality are found in his first vision at Loyola,
in the statues and shrines that sustained his devotion (Arán-
zazu, Montserrat), and in the two pictures that hung in his
study and private chapel. While, however, the 'Marian'
contemplations emphasize the infancy, they amount in their
totality to many episodes of Mary's motherhood up to and
beyond Jesus' death. Moreover, to have a sense of the
meaning of Mary's motherhood for Ignatius, we must
remember especially the place of Mary as mother beside
her Risen Son in glory [Exx. 98]. The importance of
Mary's motherhood for Ignatius lies not primarily,
however, in the dignity bestowed on Mary herself. This is
a consequence of its more fundamental importance, which
is to establish the reality of Christ's incarnation, the real
humanness of God in Christ. Thus, Christ, whether in his
mortal life or in his here-and-now glory, or in his
Eucharistic presence, is always the son to Mary of
Nazareth in Bethlehem. 'I saw and perceived clearly, that
the flesh of the mother was in the flesh of the son.'[19] For
ourselves, one important consequence of Mary's motherhood of Jesus is that it gives her the unique relationship
with him which is the basis of her special relationship to
us as mediator.

But as though to protect the motherhood of Mary in relation to Christ, Ignatius never refers to 'our' or 'my'

[19] 'Spiritual Diary', entry for 15 February, 1544, *Ignatius of Loyola:
      Personal Writings*, p. 78.

mother, in connection with Mary's motherhood, in relation
to ourselves, though he does use the word 'mother' alone
of situations where Mary exercises a maternal role in relation to other people [Exx. 199, 276]. But if 'mother'
focuses on Mary's relationship with Jesus (which is the
basis of her relationship with ourselves), the title 'Our
Lady' focuses on Mary's relationship with ourselves (of
which her motherhood of Jesus is the basis).

Of all the Marian titles, 'Our Lady' is the one employed
most frequently in the *Exercises*; it is the title always used
in the Materials for Contemplation [Exx. 261–312], except
when direct quotation requires the name of Mary. It would
be out of place to attempt to define the implications of an
expression heavy with the associations of centuries of
popular devotion; and in any case Mary could hardly be
called 'ours' if there were not a scope for every individual
to discover their own relationship with Mary and their own
image. Where the *Exercises* are concerned, it should be
noted that that the term 'Our Lady' implies the personal
human relationship with Mary as revealed in the Gospels,
and the affective quality characteristic of traditional devotion, while the expression also carries reverential overtones
corresponding to Ignatius' strong sense of Mary as
*Theotóko*s, her role in salvation history, and her present
exalted position with her Son in glory. Though in the
course of the *Exercises* attention moves from one aspect to
another of Mary's role and personality, she is always for
Ignatius at once and inseparably the Mother of Jesus and
'Our Lady' [Exx. 109].

Mary as Mediator

Though the word 'mediator' does not occur in the *Exer-
cises*, the mediation of Mary in 'obtaining graces from her
Son and Lord' [Exx. 63] is a central strand. Elsewhere in
Ignatius' writings the theme reappears, notably in connec-
tion with the decision process chronicled in the *Spiritual
Diary*, where the word 'mediator' is frequently used of

Mary.[20] In the *Reminiscences*, there is an echo of the *Exercises* in Ignatius' account of his repeated prayer to Mary for the grace 'to be placed with her son'; and at the close of his life story, he recalls numerous occasions when Our Lady had 'interceded' for him.

Today, when the *Exercises* are frequently given on an inter-Church basis, it may be especially necessary to guard this central theme from misunderstanding by making it clear that no title of Mary 'takes away from the dignity and power of Christ the one mediator, and adds nothing to this'.[21] It would be a misunderstanding of the *Exercises*, indeed of the mediating role of Mary, to think that we need in Mary a supplementary human advocate.

The keys to interpreting the mediation of Mary are the communion of saints and the unity of the Body of Christ, within which the implications of Mary's particular relationship to Christ are to be understood. We are saved not in isolation but as members of a body, a communion, and because of this all members co-operate in working out the salvation of each other. One way in which they do this is by exemplifying to one another – which is itself a kind of mediating – the Christ-life through its particular forms in our own qualities. Mainly, however, mediation means *intercession* (the word commonly used of the ordinary Christian practice of praying for one another). As used of the human being and God, the words do not imply that we need in any human being, even Mary, a kind of secondary mediator between ourselves and the Father, or that only through another human being as go-between can we approach Christ himself. We need no other mediator with God than Christ, and we need no mediator through whom

---

20 For example, 8 February, 'I desired to make this offering to the Father through the mediation and prayers of the Mother and Son. Firstly I prayed her to assist me before her Son and Father', *Personal Writings*, 'Spiritual Diary', p. 74.

21 Vatican II: Dogmatic Constitution, *Lumen gentium*, §62, (ed.) N. Tanner, *Decrees of the Ecumenical Councils,* vol. 2, London and Washington, 1990, p. 895.

to approach Christ himself, but Christ who saves us as members of his body takes into his own mediating action the prayers of those concerned for us. Within this dispensation, Mary's unique position in two respects gives particular significance to her mediation. As exemplar she is sinless. As the one who prays for and supports us, her position as the Mother who gave the world its saviour confers on her a unique sharing in Jesus' own mediation.

The function of Mary in the Triple Colloquy is deliberately reminiscent of that of a go-between with a person of great eminence, a friend at court,[22] but the analogy of courtly protocol is both enlightening and misleading. It does not mean that in relation to ourselves Jesus is, as it were, too important to be approached directly; nor does it mean that his dignity would be undermined by direct communication. The presence of Mary underlines the solemnity and seriousness of a situation, and does mean that in our relationship with Jesus we have her companionship; also that as Jesus is always Mary's son and always in his mother's presence, so we in approaching him approach the son who is always with the mother, but not as the only possible way of getting favours from Jesus, or that this kind of procedure is ever necessary. The point is that it brings home to us the seriousness of our request; it involves us with Jesus' mother who is always there; and it means that we approach Jesus with an exemplar who shows us the Christ-life in a person like us.

---

[22] A good example of Ignatius' own approach is to be found in his Spiritual Diary: e.g. 8 February, 'I desired to make this offering to the Father through the mediation and prayers of the Mother and Son. Firstly I prayed her to assist me before her Son and Father', *Personal Writings*, 'Spiritual Diary', p. 74.

Mysticism

In the broadest sense, 'mysticism' means any kind of experiential union with the absolute. However, in Catholic
tradition 'mysticism' refers to a supernatural awareness –
beyond the realm of our natural (graced) capacity – of
God's presence to (and action in) oneself. This tradition
makes certain distinctions: mysticism is distinguished from
the ascetical way which must always precede it and which
was regarded as the ordinary mode of Christian life. Mysticism contains a process, a journey, which can be said to
begin when *prayer has the quality of 'infused contemplation', and which passes through degrees of ever more
profound purification and transformation, as classified and
described by writers such as St Teresa of Avila and St John
of the Cross. There is also the important distinction
between the mysticism of the negative and the positive way
('apophatic' and 'cataphatic' mysticism described below).

Prevailing attitudes towards the mystical are constantly
changing, and it can be said today that in its current development the above tradition would tend not to consider the
mystical as unusual, but on the contrary the way in which
the ordinary Christian is led by the *Holy Spirit. Moreover,
while recognizing the distinction between the mystical and
the ascetical, there is an implicit mysticism of ordinary life.

That Ignatius was himself one of the most gifted mystics
of the Church's history is today generally accepted, but to
appreciate Ignatius the mystic it must be recognized that in
addition to the general characteristics mentioned above, the
personal mysticism of Ignatius and that of the *Exercises*
exhibit certain characteristics which differ from stereotypes
of the mystic, both past and present. Two of these characteristics particularly call for mention: Ignatian mysticism is
'positive' (*cataphatic*); and it is a mysticism of *service.

The first characteristic must be emphasized because there
can be no true appreciation of Ignatian mysticism if a positive mysticism is viewed (as today there is a tendency to
view it) as being less 'pure' and of a lower order than nega-

tive mysticism. Ignatius knows God, as does every mystic, as the Other, the always greater. But his approach to God is through intellect and sense, which are in a way transparent to realities beyond themselves, rather than through the paradoxes of darkness and absence. It is also important, in view of ordinary ideas of mysticism, to stress that for Ignatius mystical union culminates not in the union of the mind in contemplation, but in union of the will in the service of the Kingdom and the frequent choices required by that service.[23]

The *Exercises* are 'mystical' in the sense that, whatever might be the exercitant's initial level of spiritual giftedness, they are open to – and conduce to – the expansion of this into realms of deep union. This is particularly apparent in two features of the *Exercises*: (i) anticipated, but not of course guaranteed, *experiences* of God's action described in connection with Election and *consolation;[24] and (ii) the key *desires*, especially to participate in Christ's *poverty,[25] to experience all reality in its relationship to God,[26] to experience an interior suffering and joy, which are participations in Christ's Paschal mystery.[27]

Paschal mystery

Through the sending of the Spirit we become sharers in the passion, death, and resurrection of Christ, 'dying' progressively to sin and to all that impedes new life in Christ, and

---

23 This is summed up in the *Constitutions* by the phrase *instrumentum conjunctum*, the 'conjoined instrument': 'For the preservation and development not only of the body or exterior of the Society but also of its spirit, and for the attainment of the objective it seeks, which is to aid souls to reach their ultimate and supernatural end, the means which *unite the human instrument with God* and so dispose it that it may be wielded dexterously by His divine hand are more effective than those which equip it in relation to men', *Constitutions* Part X, 2 [§813] (tr., Ganss, p. 332).
24 [Exx. 15, 175, 316, 330].
25 [Exx. 146, 167].
26 [Exx. 233].
27 [Exx. 48, 203, 221].

entering progressively into a transformation of self, which is the beginning of our full participation in Christ's life in his Kingdom. This process, which comes about through every aspect of our following of Christ and our search for God's will, is known as the 'Paschal mystery'.

The term itself entered into general circulation after the Vatican II Council, where it figures in the Decree on the liturgy.[28] But though the term is not to be found in Ignatius' writings, the concept is basic to his spiritual outlook. In particular, it provides the key to the character of the Third and Fourth Week contemplations of the *Exercises*, and to the way in which these contemplations carry over into the exercitant's subsequent life. The grace of these Weeks is not only to be *present to* these events, but to *share in* them [Exx. 48], suffering with Christ suffering [Exx. 203], and rejoicing with Christ in joy [Exx. 221, 229]. In this way one enters at the level of contemplative experience into the essential meaning for human life of the passion, death, and resurrection of Jesus, his ascension and sending of the Spirit. In the exercitant's subsequent life, what is lived in the *Exercises*, in intense contemplation, is lived out in daily prayer, in the ordinary disciplines of spiritual growth, in the choices and acceptances of doing God's will, and especially through the way of humility set out in the Two Standards [Exx. 146], and meeting the call of the King to share in Christ's labour and suffering 'that they may also follow me into glory' [Exx. 95].[29]

---

[28]   'The great divine acts among the people of the old covenant foreshadowed this deed of human redemption and perfect glorification of God; Christ the Lord brought it to its completion, above all through the paschal mystery, that is, his passion, his resurrection from the dead and his glorious ascension', Vatican II, *Sacrosanctum concilium* [Constitution on the sacred liturgy], Preamble, §2 [Tanner, *Decrees*, p. 820].

[29]   Cf. 'we were buried therefore with him by baptism into death, so that as Christ was raised from the dead by the glory of the Father, we too might walk in newness of life', Romans 6:4.

Apophatic/Cataphatic Mysticism

Apophatic mysticism is based on the principle that God and creatures are so unlike that God is more truly found in a contemplation without concepts, words or images; while in cataphatic, or positive mysticism, contemplation goes through these to the *reality* beyond them. The apophatic way is typified by darkness, the cataphatic by transparency. The apophatic, to the fore in the spiritual tradition of the Christian East, is associated in the West especially with Eckhart, the English anonymous author of the *Cloud of Unknowing*, and St John of the Cross. Cataphatic mysticism finds one of its main exemplars in Ignatius.

The types of contemplation characteristic of these two kinds of mysticism differ from one another considerably, but the distinction is not one of total discontinuity. If authentic, both apophatic and cataphatic mysticism contain elements of the other and each can challenge the other's tendencies to inauthenticity. Thus apophatic contemplation is prepared for by meditation; outside of contemplation, apophatic spirituality continues to be supported and nourished by Scripture, tradition, the community, the Church, etc. As regards cataphatic spirituality it must be stressed that this is not limited to discursive prayer; the intrinsic dynamic of cataphatic contemplation moves to the simple and receptive, as for instance in the prayer of the *Exercises* centred on a single contemplated word [Exx. 249] or sense object [Exx. 125]. Moreover, the fact that a person's ordinary contemplation is cataphatic does not preclude fully apophatic moments (for Ignatius such a moment was the Cardoner enlightenment).

Both spiritualities are ways of love, a point needing perhaps to be stressed against tendencies to equate Christian contemplation simply with 'emptying the mind'. And as ways of receiving and responding to God's love, neither has any superiority over the other.

Truly mystical?

Not all exponents of the *Exercises* have, however, accepted their mystical orientation. While the mystical quality of Ignatius as a person is recognized, there are some who would see in the *Exercises* a programme and doctrine from which the mystical is even excluded. Various factors explain such a view. Thus, the mysticism of the *Exercises*, like that of Ignatius himself, will always put a problem to people who see the apophatic model as the higher or purer, or whose concept of the mystical does not easily accommodate the idea of a '*service' mysticism. Failure to recognize the mystical dimension of the *Exercises* can also result from the very nature of the book itself: the fact that it is a director's manual, which leaves much to be discovered by the exercitant in a personal way, that critical points of spiritual doctrine are often touched on only in single sentences or phrases; above all, that the *Exercises* are not a treatise on mysticism, and do not enter into the distinctions of mystical theology. Finally, the image of the *Exercises* as an ascetical manual owes something to the Jesuits themselves, repeatedly anxious to avoid any involvement with suspect 'mystical' movements. This tendency is already apparent in the 1599 Directory.

Poverty

Three prayers of petition run through the Second Week of the *Exercises*: to be admitted to the 'highest spiritual poverty', to be chosen for 'actual poverty' should this be God's wish, and to incur '*contempt and opprobrium', should this be possible without another's sin or displeasure to the Divine Majesty.[30] These *graces represent a conversion of outlook and *desire which Ignatius considered integral to all growth in Christ. They are his way of defining the difference between an ordinary and 'reasonable' [Exx. 96] following of Christ and the following of radical discipleship. To many people today, however, desire for poverty and opprobrium may seem an excessively constricted, not to say socially and psychologically dubious, way of summarising radical Christian dispositions. Hence the text is likely to require clarification and a modicum of commentary if an exercitant today is to discover its real meaning and personal application.

Poverty: 'spiritual'/'actual'

How is the distinction between 'spiritual' and 'actual' poverty to be understood? Spiritual poverty, for which the exercitant prays unconditionally, consists in a Christ-centred attitude that transforms a person's experience of all reality and the quality of their entire commerce with it. Its effects combine humility with the freedom of indifference; hence the spiritually poor accept all things from God, making use of and enjoying God's creatures according to God's will. They are non-possessive people, who if they have possessions, are not possessed by them.[31] As an attitude, spiritual poverty does not require absolutely that a

---

30 Note the change of order between the offering in the Kingdom (insult and abuse, actual poverty, spiritual poverty [Exx. 98]) and the Triple Colloquy of the Two Standards (spiritual poverty, actual poverty, humiliations and insults [Exx. 147]). The Kingdom offering begins with the situation that for an honour-conscious sixteenth-century exercitant would probably have been the most immediately challenging.

31 'It rather behooves you to reflect that, if you have possessions, they not possess you, nor should you be possessed by anything temporal, but should refer them all to the Master from whom you have received them', *Letter to Pietro Contarini* [a Venetian nobleman and cleric], MHSI *Epistolae S. Ignatii*, I (Madrid, 1903), pp. 124–5; original in Latin, English translation William J. Young, p. 32.

person be in 'actual poverty'. It does, nevertheless, contain
an openness to actual poverty, sets value on it, positively
desires, in some profound sense, to be called to it.

While spiritual poverty is an attitude, 'actual poverty' is
a situation. It is a situation always in some way marked by
real loss or diminishment or in some sense corresponding
to the concept of 'insults and injuries'; hence it is always a
situation antithetical to that of 'riches and honour'. But not
every situation describable in these terms falls under the
'actual poverty' of the *Exercises*. For one thing, the *Exercises* are concerned only with 'voluntary' poverty, that is to
say a poverty either chosen or at least freely accepted as
personally meaningful. Moreover, actual poverty is to be
understood as a participation in the poverty exemplified and
recommended by Christ, as an embodiment therefore of the
Christ-given attitude of poverty of spirit. In relation to the
Exercises three implications of this should be specially
noted:

(i) through poverty one is made free from the cupidity that
leads to *pride, and brought by and with Christ into the
personal quality of *humility [Exx. 145-146];

(ii) the effects of poverty are both personal and apostolic;
through poverty the follower of Christ is present in the
world in a way that builds the kingdom of God (the poor
in Christ belong to and build the New Jerusalem, while
the place of the rich and proud is with Babylon);

(iii) actual poverty, though real, entails no diminution of the
positive theology of *creation basic to the *Exercises* [Exx.
144].

There are countless ways in practice in which actual
poverty, thus understood, might assume concrete forms. In
the *Exercises* pride of place goes to the poverty in which
non-possessiveness of attitude finds expression in a poverty
of literal non-possession. Thus, an exercitant might become
'actually poor' as a result, for example, of turning down a
benefice or an inheritance; and belonging to a category of
its own in the *Exercises* is the radical and pre-eminent form

of actual poverty which constitutes a '*state' or life situation [Exx. 98]. But it must also be kept in mind that the
special place given by Ignatius to poverty as a 'state', and
to the distinction between the way of evangelical perfection
and that of the commandments does not exclude other ways
the follower of Christ might be called to participate in the
poverty of Christ by translating 'spiritual' into 'actual'
poverty.

Poverty as a 'state' (a dimension of life)

An exercitant of the time, especially one seeking a way of
life, would have known quite well what the *Exercises* meant
in referring to poverty as a 'state'. Belonging to the state
of poverty were those who through the course of history
had received and responded to the same call as was
addressed to the Apostles and the rich young man – to
abandon all possessions in order to throw in their lot with
Christ and the service of his kingdom (cf. [Exx. 97–98]).
In the culture of the time, response to such a call would
ordinarily take the form of entering a religious order, especially an order practising mendicancy with its inbuilt
dependency on Providence.

In the *Exercises*, centred as they are round the discernment of a personal life-vocation, poverty in this sense is
much to the fore, and indeed Ignatius' concern to maintain
its distinctive character means that in the *Exercises* we find
no *explicit* application of the concept of 'actual poverty' to
Christian life as such. Even in the sections which touch on
the use and disposal of resources in everyday life [Exx. 189
and 344) the word 'poor', though applied to the lifestyle
deemed desirable for a bishop [Exx. 344], is not used in
connection with the Christian lay person. This does not,
however, warrant a division of Christ's followers into a
minority chosen for actual poverty of a specific form and a
majority for whom poverty is 'spiritual' only, with any
aspiration to the 'actual' never in any substantial sense to
be realized. Such a division hardly fits the language of the

Two Standards, with its insistence that the 'sacred doctrine'
of Christ is to be spread among people of *every state and
condition*. The vision which gives the 'state of poverty' its
meaning has implications, therefore, for everyone; and
hence the colloquies of the Two Standards can be interpreted not only as the request of a person at a moment of
life-choice to be called to poverty as a 'state', but also as
the request of a person wishing to be radically Christ-like
to share in the poverty of Christ in whatever (possibly
unforeseeable) ways the Father might grant.

This wider concept of poverty does not imply that radical
discipleship can preclude the possibility of poverty in a
literal, material guise. But understood more widely the
concept of poverty can extend to any situation of loss or
diminishment or any situation antithetical to what might for
a particular individual constitute 'riches or honour'.
Whether they arise from action or risk or occur unavoid-
ably, such situations, if they are willed or accepted in faith,
can be matter for the association with Christ in poverty that
leads both to a deepening personal assimilation and to apostolic witness.

From the Exercises *to daily Life*

Voluntary poverty, both as a practice and a realm of
meaning, must be set in relation not only to the Gospel but
also to the circumstances and culture of the individual or
group who adopt it. The *Exercises* deal with poverty mainly
on the level of essential principles.

Where Ignatius himself is concerned, a detailed picture
of the constants, variables and tensions of the lived poverty
of a sixteenth-century apostolic order is provided by the
Jesuit *Constitutions* and other early Jesuit documents, and
fully to understand Ignatius' own vision of poverty recourse
to these sources is essential. In living on the basis of that
vision today, account must also be taken of developments
in outlook and changes of situation that have come about
since the sixteenth century. For example, in religious life,

the practice of begging, in Ignatius' time a routine necessity of life in a Jesuit residence, is no longer considered
unambiguously edifying,[32] and many other traditional
forms of poverty are called in question as artificial, merely
juridical, unrealistic or inconsistent with a current theology
of the world. On the other hand, contemporary awareness
of an interconnected and intrinsically changeable world and
of corresponding personal and corporate responsibilities
leads many today to find inspiration in the ideals of a
counter-cultural witness in the face of today's cupidity, and
also to sharing in some way in Christ's own commitment to
those who are poor without choice. At the same time, with
the decline of fundamentalist attitudes, people today more
readily appreciate that poverty takes many other forms than
those of material or economic want. In this complex situation new partialities, tensions and conflicts arise and
through these the individual must discern his or her own
position before the ways set out in the Two Standards meditation. For many people making the *Exercises* today the
prayer for actual poverty might consist most effectively in
taking the risk in faith of asking to be involved in the
poverty of Christ, to walk according to the paradoxes of the
Beatitudes, in whatever way should be according to Christ's
wish and choice.

[32] 'The style of life, prayer and work of the modern religious should
reflect contemporary ideas and living standards. It must too, as far as
the character of each institute allows, respond to the demands of the
apostolate, cultural patterns and the prevailing social and economic
climate, particularly in missionary territories',Vatican II: Decree on the
sensitive renewal of religious life (*Perfectae caritatis*), §3 (ed.) N.
Tanner, *Decrees of the Ecumenical Councils,* vol. 2, London 1990,
p. 940.

Religious Life

While there are people able to live in chosen poverty and
chastity, who would be ill-advised to live in community or
under obedience, the normal way of living the counsels was
held in Ignatius' time to be 'religious life'.[33] Working on
these assumptions, Ignatius proposes that when an exercitant
has made a choice for the counsels, he or she should go on to
consider, step by step, three remaining elements of choice:

> (i) should they follow the counsels within or outside reli-
> gious life?
> (ii) if religious life is chosen, does the Lord invite one more
> to a life of retirement or more to imitating himself in
> gaining souls?
> (iii) when to put the decision into execution?[34]

The *Exercises* incorporate in their very structure Ignatius'
understanding of religious life as a *service into which God
calls men and women throughout history as the Apostles
were called [Exx. 175, 275]; and especially, though implicitly, the *Exercises* commend Ignatius' own concept of
apostolic religious life. But he is concerned that no pressure be brought to bear on an exercitant to choose religious
life, and he insists that such a choice, if made, be made
freely and from a right *intention. Thus, in the course of
the *Exercises* the director should make no attempt to
persuade a retreatant to enter religious life [Exx. 15], and
an exercitant of suspect enthusiasm or judgement must be
warned against rushing into religious life [Exx. 336]. In
connection with religious *vocation the *Directories* enlist
the image of the tower builder of Luke's Gospel (Luke 14:
28–30):[35] a vocation implies not only the impulse to

---

33 *Directories*: 'the counsels can nowadays hardly be followed outside reli-
    gious life', Official Directory, ch. 25, 3 (§180), Palmer p. 328; cp.
    Directory of Fr Dávila (§112), Palmer p. 254. The term 'religious life'
    refers specifically to life in an order or congregation.
34 *Directories* as in the previous note.
35 *Directories*: Directory of Fr Dávila (§110), Palmer p. 254.

conceive a project, but the resources – mainly a *desire for God's glory – to see it through. Dávila also draws attention to the disastrous consequences of having people in religious life who have no aptitude for it.[36]

It should also be noted that Ignatius was concerned that the impression should never be given that people who make the *Exercises* finish by entering religious life: 'it is fear of the idea that they will end up by entering religion, or that only religious and similar persons make the *Exercises* which frequently renders people reluctant to make them'.[37]

Soul

According to the standard usage of his time Ignatius uses the term 'soul' either to designate the spiritual component of the human person, or, more generally, as simply synonymous with 'person'. Though today the word 'soul' easily causes uneasiness, we need to realize that when we find the term used in the past in ways we would now avoid as implying a dualistic attitude, this does not necessarily imply that any such implications were carried in the past. Ignatian spirituality, indeed, is characterized by a strong sense of the whole person and by considerable respect for the *body. Salvation of one's 'soul' means, therefore, the salvation, the ultimate fulfilment, of the whole person. But if 'saving one's soul' does not imply an 'anti-body' attitude, it does draw attention to the fact that the ultimate fulfilment

---

[36] *Directories*: Directory of Fr Dávila (§34), Palmer p. 238.
[37] *Directories*: Directory dictated by Ignatius to Juan Alonso de Vitoria (§3), Palmer, p. 17.

of the whole person is to be found only by following values which are *more than* the immediate and material.

In the *Exercises* expressions such as 'save my soul' or 'salvation of the soul' are used in a distinctive way, usually found as part of a wider statement of the 'end' for which we are created (and hence the norm on which choices should be made), and affirming that fulfilment of the human person lies in a gift of union with God. Strikingly, in such statements the reference to personal salvation always occurs in second place to objectives such as '*glory', '*service', 'praise' of God. Personal salvation on the one hand, praise, glory and service on the other, are inseparable aspects of a single call. Each implies the other. Yet the order in which they are stated is an important indicator of Ignatius' spiritual attitude. Religious language can sometimes give the impression that God is a *means* to the saving of one's soul; and while the first lines of the Principle and Foundation ('The human person is created to praise, reverence and serve God our Lord, and by so doing save his or her soul' [Exx. 23]) might seem to say this, especially if taken out of context, Ignatius' soul-language is in no way yoked to this kind of interpretation. What comes first expresses what might be termed an attitude of radically self-forgetful God-centredness, the concern that God be God in his world and in one's life, that his 'Kingdom come and his will be done'. It is an attitude that contrasts strongly with the self-absorption, the juridical and sometimes minimalist attitude of Christians concerned only to 'save their souls'. Yet there remains the inalienable responsibility to co-operate in the work of one's own salvation and to embrace the personal discipline this might require, and hence comes Ignatius' practice of adding the more *personal* criterion to the more immediately theocentric one.

Powers of the soul

As a spiritual being, the human person acts and is acted upon through the three 'powers of the soul', memory, understanding and will (the faculty of love and desire). To appreciate the significance of the 'powers' in the *Exercises* it is important to be aware that they belong to a tradition which sees the powers as the means of exchange between ourselves and God. On our side through their 'right use' we seek God, but we 'use' them also in order to sin. While on God's side they are the material of his action in transforming and drawing us into his life, in sin, conversely, we misuse the powers of the soul: sin enters into and contaminates the personality. Thus, to quote a typical mediaeval authority: through sin, 'Forgetfulness damages the remembrance of God, our knowledge of Him becomes clouded with error, and our love is narrowed down to selfish lust', while through Christ, 'the image of God within us is perfectly reformed, when forgetfulness no longer falsifies memory, when knowledge has no error to confuse it, and love is free of cupidity'.[38]

In the *Exercises* the powers of the soul are referred to by name in the First Meditation (on the Three Sins [Exx. 45, 51]) and in the First Way of Prayer [Exx. 238, 246]; they also constitute the matter of the prayer of offering in the *Contemplatio ad amorem* ('Take Lord and receive all my liberty, my memory, my understanding and my entire will ...' [Exx. 234]). In the First Meditation the deployment of the three powers is more than a psychological technique: one prays in the hope and confidence that in the very method God himself will act in and through the faculties by which we seek him – enabling us to call to mind (*memory*) his earlier word to us, to *understand* it with the light of the Spirit, so as to be led to 'interior knowledge',[39] to experience in the *will* a graced desire and impetus to service. In the First Way of Prayer one seeks a 'perfect understanding' [Exx. 240] of the powers, while one practices a certain scrutiny of one's use of them. In the *Contemplatio* it is precisely the powers of the soul, with special emphasis on

---

38 St Aelred, *The Mirror of Charity*, cc. 4–5, p. 7.
39 'For it is not much knowledge but the inner feeling and relish of things that fills and satisfies the soul' [Exx. 2].

freedom, that are handed over to God, so that he take them over and dispose of them according to his will.

While named explicitly only in these texts, the powers of the soul operate, though not all at a level of consciousness, in all *prayer.

State of life

The word 'state' occurs about a dozen times[40] in the *Exercises* and is sometimes linked to 'life',[41] which serves to add connotations of process, dynamism and personal quality to the otherwise over static implications of 'state'. The term refers particularly to the ways of the counsels and of the commandments [Exx. 135], and to situations and commitments based on these, or on sacramental status: priesthood, *religious life, chosen single life, *marriage. More generally the term refers – but always with the nuance of permanence – to the whole diversity of ministries in the Church.[42]

Although Ignatius distinguishes between the way of the counsels (which he sees as 'higher') and the way of the Commandments, this should not be taken to mean that all are not called to 'perfection'. On the contrary the purpose of the *Exercises* is to find perfection in whatever state of life one is called to [Exx. 135].[43]

---

40 Thus, [Exx. 15, 40, 98, 135, 141, 145, 154, 177, 189, 339, 343, 344]; probably the word is not used by Ignatius to signify a political State or nation, but some doubt remains, cf. [Exx. 141, 145]

41 [Exx. 98, 135, 177, 343].

42 *Directories* (Official Directory of 1599, §164), p. 324.

43 [This short paragraph is all that appears in the papers on the theme of 'Perfection', even if in the List (see Introduction) it is included among the 'Nearly Complete'.]

Ignatius never limited the *Exercises* to persons faced with the need to choose a state in life, but he was emphatic that this was a particularly suitable situation in which to make them, for two reasons:

(i) such a choice was not simply one choice among many, but had a critical importance of its own. As the Official Directory of 1599 explains, if all actions should be directed to a supernatural end, this must be especially the case with the act of choosing a state of life; for on this state almost every action of our life will depend, and hence if the end is faulty, all that depend on it will necessarily be faulty as well.[44]

(ii) while being an important issue in itself, the choice of a state of life also tended to favour the very process of the *Exercises* by exposing the exercitant to the 'diversity of spirits'.[45]

To people today the term 'state' may suggest more stable and stratified models of the Church and society than ours; but the principle embodied in the word is of crucial importance – that within the general condition of baptized membership of the believing community, individuals are called to find God, both in their inner lives and in their *service to the world.

Trinity

Ignatius' spirituality, both his personal and that promoted by the *Exercises*, is characterized by a Trinitarian

---

[44] See Note 42.
[45] *Directories* (*Memoriale* of Gonçalves da Câmara, quoting Ignatius, §3), p. 29.

consciousness. The mystical 'education'[46] he received at
Manresa begins with a vision of the Trinity which, even
more than an infused communication of doctrine, was an
overwhelming, and permanently transforming, experience.[47] From that moment, explicitly Trinitarian *prayer
was habitual in his life, and the *Spiritual Diary* testifies to
the specific forms this could take.[48] In the First Contemplation of the Second Week of the Exercises the drama of
human history is set in relation to the divine Persons in a
graphic picture: 'to recall the history of the subject to be
contemplated: in this case how the three divine Persons
were looking down upon the face and circuit of the world,
filled with people' [Exx. 102].

In Ignatius' Trinitarian theology the Trinity is seen not
only as the final revelation of God's being and life, but of
God's creating and saving action in the world (hence, in tech-
nical terminology, as both the 'immanent' and 'economic'
Trinity). The action of the Trinity is understood as a pattern
of descent and ascent by which *all things come from the
Trinitarian God and return to that God. The perception of all
reality in relation to this movement is generally considered
the key to the Cardoner enlightenment.[49]

The Trinitarian spirituality of Ignatius is also Christo-
centric. Christ's saving entry into the world is the decision
of the Trinity; his mission is that of the Trinity [Exx. 102].
Sent by the Trinity, he empties himself to enter and to die
in and for the world (cf. the first mention of Christ in the
Exercises),[50] and so to bring all creation back to God.

46 'At this time God was dealing with him in the same way as a school-
teacher deals with a child, teaching him', *Personal Writings*,
'Reminiscences' §27, p. 25.
47 *Personal Writings*, 'Reminiscences' §28, p. 25.
48 *Personal Writings*, numerous references in the *Spiritual Diary* especially between 18 February and 12 March, p. 81–99.
49 *Personal Writings*, 'Reminiscences' §30 describing his spiritual experience as he sat on the bank of the River Cardoner, pp. 26–7.
50 The so-called colloquy of the *cross that closes the First Meditation of
the First Week: '... make a colloquy asking how it came about that the
Creator made himself a human being and from eternal life came to
temporal death, and thus to die for my sins' [Exx. 53].

Every mystery contemplated in the *Exercises* is a moment in this pattern.

The movement of Christ to the Father is the principle of the process of continuing personal conversion (in which in the *Exercises* the Trinitarian triple *colloquies are crucial moments). It is also the principle of Christ's mission in the world. For Ignatius, Trinitarian sprituality is therefore essentially apostolic. In the experiences of his own life, this is highlighted in the vision at La Storta where Ignatius is enlisted into the crucified apostolic service of the Father and the Son – an event which he saw as the answer to his prayer 'to be placed with the Son'.[51] In the *Exercises*, Ignatius would have the exercitant contemplate the Trinity not in a way that leads to oblivion of the world, but in a way that invites participation in God's own compassionate vision of the human race, and collaboration with Christ in the work of his kingdom.

The apostolic character of Ignatius Trinitarian spirituality gives rise to a particular emphasis regarding the Spirit, who is the source of discernment, of insight into truths of faith, of right decision-making, of judgement. Thus, in the Preface to the Jesuit *Constitutions*, he writes: 'the law of the Spirit, written onto the hearts of the faithful, is a more fundamental guide than written Constitutions'.[52] On a cursory reading, it may appear, however, that the *Exercises* fail to give full prominence to the *Spirit, explicit references being found only in the Gospel summaries [Exx. 263, 273, 304, 307, 312] and the Rules for thinking with the Church [Exx. 365]. It is possible, but by no means beyond question, that in his explicit references to the *Holy Spirit (as mentioned above) Ignatius deliberately chose restraint in order to avoid charges of illuminism. Be this as it may, the Spirit is to the fore wherever the *Exercises* deal with the effects of the Spirit (enlightenment [Exx. 2], 'intimate feelings and relish' [Exx. 2], 'courage and strength' [Exx. 315]), in all the ways of deci-

---

51 *Personal Writings*, 'Reminiscences' §96, p. 60.
52 *Constitutions*, Preamble, 1 [§134] (Ganss, p. 119).

sion-making, and in every reference to *consolation, in its
various forms, and to the 'good sprit' (*el buen espíritu*) [Exx.
32, 314, 318, 336]. In connection with the Trinity, as always
when discussing a theological dimension of Ignatius' spirituality, we must bear in mind that he is not a systematic theologian and that much of his doctrine is implicit rather than
explicit. The director today should not be hesitant about
making explicit the Trinitarian implications of the *Exercises*,
many of which correspond to more developed positions of
contemporary theology.

Vocation

The word '*vocación*' ('vocation') occurs in the *Exercises* to
refer to the specific 'states of life' or particular offices or
ministries that might be chosen by an exercitant.[53] To
choose a *state of life, as the process is understood in the
Exercises, is to respond to a vocation, or call. To put the
matter another way, what is 'choice' on the part of the
exercitant is 'vocation' on the side of God – the vocation to
a specific state or ministry within the general call extended
to all men and women.

Ignatius does not attempt a comprehensive treatment of
vocation but deals with the subject in relation to an exercitant choosing a state in life in an *election situation, i.e. a
person exteriorly and interiorly free in relation to alterna-

---

53   In connection with 'immutable' choices, see [Exx. 171, 172]. The idea
     of a more general *vocación* ('call') is strongly present: Christ's univer-
     sal call to the service of the kingdom [Exx. 95], and to true life in
     Christ [Exx. 137]; the call of the Apostles [Exx. 275], and in the
     context of Election [Exx. 175].

tive options, and who, at least consciously, wishes to reach a decision on the sole criterion of God's greater *service. In the mind of such a person he wants to establish the idea of vocation as a 'personal call', an idea little in general view in his time. Such a person must also be aware that each of the options could be God's will for him or her personally, but that it is easy to claim a motivation far removed from the self-interest by which one is in fact controlled.[54] From this standpoint, he considers it particularly important to set down three broad principles: first, a divine vocation is totally limpid and free from contamination by self-interested motivation; second, people who have made an oblique and wrong choice cannot claim to be where they are in consequence of a vocation, and he specifically deplores the widespread assumption to the contrary; third, in the case of people in an unchangeable state,[55] as a result of an improperly made election, there is no other legitimate option than to repent and lead a good life in their situation.

All three statements must be interpreted in relation to the *Exercises* and to their original setting. Set in relation to the *Exercises*, the quality of motivation required for an authentic vocation corresponds precisely to the initial definition of their objective – to make a decision not determined by some disordered *affection;[56] and the basic assumption of the *Exercises* is that choices of this quality are possible because they are the actions of a mind and will influenced and enlightened by the *Holy Spirit and open to a Spirit-given potential. To avoid the impression that Ignatius claims even

54   Ignatius points out in a Note [Exx. 174] that an election may 'not have been made sincerely and in due order', in which case 'it will be to one's profit to make the election properly'.
55   By 'unchangeable state' he refers not only to priesthood and *marriage but also to professed religious life, from which release was not at the time considered possible.
56   At the beginning of the First Week he defines the 'purpose' of the *Exercises* as 'the overcoming of self and the ordering of one's life on the basis of a decision made in freedom from any disordered attachment' [Exx. 21].

more than he does, it should be noted, however, that freedom from disordered affection does not require a mind totally empty of such affections, only that *to no degree* do they enter a person's motives for choice. It should also be noted that the qualities of a true vocation appear not only, or even usually, in a Damascus road experience [Exx. 175]; they can be the outcome of Second and Third Time discernment, possibly prolonged over processes of search that may well exceed the scope of the *Exercises*.

Reference to oblique and wrong choices would obviously have been pertinent to innumerable career clerics of the time, but not everyone in a state of life not coming out of a 'good and true election' had necessarily made a personally 'disordered or wrong' choice. In a society that put people into convents and monasteries as small children, and offered its women no other options than (often arranged) *marriage or the veil, there were doubtless many people who had made no personal choice at all of a life-situation. The *Exercises* need not be read as passing implicit judgement on people of this kind. They are addressed to people about to assume the responsibility of making a decision in freedom, and their concern is that these be aware of the possibility – powerfully endorsed by the climate of the times – of choosing a state of life out of self-interested reasons and rationalizing these as a divine vocation.

Of all three statements, the one most likely to strike a jarring note in the modern reader is the third, with its insistence that certain decisions once made and ratified establish an irreversible objective situation, and the seemingly minimal spiritual prospects offered to people trapped in such situation by wrong or ill-considered past decision. The principle of immutability came not from Ignatius but from the Church, and the conclusions Ignatius draws from it, which might well, of course, bear directly on the position of an exercitant, is less negative than might appear. For although Ignatius uses the word 'vocation' only of the decision to enter a state of life, not of a conversion within a state, he does not set limits to the quality of converted and graced life a person might find in a situation not originally embarked on out of love and now unchangeable. However, where initial motivation was self-interest, it is essential to 'repent', because only in this way does the original motivation cease to be a block between the individual and the generosity to God reaching out to him or her here and now.

If they are to serve as guides for today, Ignatius' positions need to be supplemented and modified in certain ways. Where immutable choice is concerned we must recognize that changes in legislation give rise today to new possibilities of decision and discernment 'within the bounds of the Church'. While Ignatius is clear that vocation as a subjective experience may not be what it seems to be,[57] we cannot ignore the developed and systematized knowledge available today about the psychological factors that can complicate the discernment of vocation. Nevertheless, in many respects the emphases of his doctrine anticipate those of today's Church – his insistence on vocation as personal call, and his sense of the scope of vocation as embracing any life situation approved by the Church.

Will of God

In the writings of Ignatius, the will (or wish) of God is associated mainly with *decision* and *action*. God's will is something one 'does'. But to appreciate the significance of

---

[57] Thus, 'if the giver sees that the exercitant is going ahead in consolation and full of fervour, the latter ought to be forewarned against making any unthinking or precipitate promise or vow', Annotation 14 [Exx. 14]; similar advice is to be found in the Rules for Discernment (e.g. [Exx. 333–334]).

God's will as the rule of choice and action, we must begin
more basically, with God's will as object of *desire. Desire
that the will of God (God's universal will for humankind
and God's will for each individual) be fulfilled in the world
and in one's own life, is implicit in the infused desires of
faith, hope and *love. In the *Exercises*, this desire is encapsulated in the *prayer in which the exercitant with much
love (*afectándose mucho* [Exx. 234]) places him or her self
entirely at the disposition of God and his will. In dealing
with the implications of doing God's will, it must be kept
in mind that the basis of doing God's will in specific
choices and actions is union with God's will in *desire*. It is
this desire which is the basis of the choices, and is embodied in them.

Will of God and decision

Doing God's will does not consist only in explicit decisions. Such is God's involvement in his own creation that
unless we expressly opt otherwise, we do God's will in the
ordinary and autonomous details of daily existence, without
necessarily thinking about the matter. Where explicit decisions are concerned, certain distinctions need to be made,
and their implications for doing God's will should be noted.

First, while every decision properly so called is an
explicit act of personal freedom, where the objects of decision in the external world are concerned, a distinction can
be drawn between decisions to *accept* and decisions to
bring about change, decisions to let something happen and
decisions to make something happen. The *Exercises*,
specially concerned as they are with collaboration in
Christ's mission in the world and with life-choices, give a
particular emphasis to action decisions. But for this very
reason it is necessary to insist on the fundamental importance of *acceptance*: acceptance of situations unchangeable
in themselves, or of a situation judged morally non-negotiable, or at least preferable, in relation to objectively
possible alternatives. To say this is not to commend atti-

tudes of fatalism or passivity, or the habit of ascribing immutability where to bring about change is eminently possible and even imperative. An authentic spirituality of God's will, requires, however, that we recognize that the supreme moments of human freedom consist precisely in acts of acceptance – ultimately the acceptance of one's own death, as, in Christ, acceptance of death was the culminating redemptive act.

A second important distinction concerns the norms and criteria by which decisions are made. There are situations where general principles, such as the word of God in scripture and tradition, objective morality, acts of authority, specific commitments and responsibilities, etc., are determinative of choice. There are also situations in which general norms, though relevant, do not close the issue. These latter belong to the space between the 'obligatory' and the 'forbidden' – where *indifference in the Ignatian sense is possible [Exx 23].

It is in relation to this latter situation that Ignatius proposes the Times of Election, the signs through which God indicates his will to one truly seeking it, the unmistakable call, tested *consolation, and the preponderant rational case.[58] It must be noted here that the 'times' are significant not only because they provide the genuine seeker with practical principles and a method, but because of their implicit assumptions: that God's will can be personal, that within the constants of the moral and Christian life there is a will of God for the individual, a unique way which is the Spirit-guided working out of each one's personal *vocation. All this does not imply that the discovery of God's will through other mediations than personal experience was considered by Ignatius less to be desired, or of lower quality than the way of discernment. We find God's will as God discloses it at any given moment. In the *Exercises*, however, Ignatius is especially concerned with decision

---

[58] A fuller treatment of the Times of Election to be found in *Understanding*, pp. 135–45; see also *election.

situations where objective criteria are not coercive, and
with the particular ways in which God's will is found in this
way.

Difficulties

Despite what has been said, it must be recognized that the
idea of taking God's will as the governing principle of life
raises considerable difficulties today – so much so that the
entire subject, for all its scriptural centrality, is widely
downplayed as an explicit theme of spirituality.

At one level these difficulties reflect another, rooted in
the human condition itself: our instinctive holding back in
relation to God's claims on us. But there are also difficulties connected with words and model. In seeking to
comprehend the relationship between the omnipotence,
freedom and initiative of God with human liberty and the
manifold aspects of human limitation, we are dealing with
a transcendent reality which necessarily eludes our full
comprehension and which can only be approached with the
help of models, which by definition are unlike, as well as
like, the reality they point to. Because our analogies are
inadequate, one analogy may need the complement of
another, and in approaching the mystery of the divine will
in relation to human reality, at least two models, both
implicit in the *Exercises*, are necessary. They might be
designated as 'initiative and discovery', on the one hand,
and 'collaboration' on the other: in one model, God is the
sole author of his decisions, and though God's decision
takes the creature fully into account, the creature's role is
simply one of assent (as in the Annunciation or the call of
the Apostles); in the other model, in some sense God's will
is the action of God in and through the action of the creature. In both models God's will is something the creature
finds, and in both the creature *assents* to what is given to
him or her. But on the first model, God's will is 'found' in
the sense in which one finds something that already exists,
in the second one 'finds' God's will as one 'finds' the

personal solution to a problem. In the first, one 'assents' to
what one has in no way participated in making; in the
second, while the creature 'assents' to the action of God at
every stage of the process, what one assents to finally is
brought about by the action of God in and through the creature's own act.

With regard to each of these models certain caveats
should be noted. For the first model, our ability to apply it
appropriately is affected by ways of understanding the term
'will' itself. For in scholastic psychology 'will' is primarily a faculty of *desire; today 'will' is associated more with
'power', rather than with the desire which is the basis of
the power. Hence in the *Exercises* the willing of God is the
wishing or desiring of God; and to 'do God's will' is to do
what is 'pleasing' to God (cf. [Exx. 151]), thus language
suggestive of a relationship of *love, freedom and mutual-
ity. Where on the other hand 'will' is associated mainly
with 'power', doing the will of another suggests the adver-
sarial and dominative, an over-against quality of
relationship.[59]

But even when we recognize that the merely dominative
connotations of the intervention model come in part from a
shift in the sense of 'will', and our assent is seen as a truly
relational assent to God's desires, a difficulty remains about
imaging the relationship between the divine and human
wills simply as one of intervention and assent. To conceive
of the ordinary events, activities and circumstances of
human life in terms of seeking and finding God's will, we
need recourse, as well, to collaboration models – the idea
of God as acting in and through our own decision-making

---

[59] Mark A. McIntosh, *Mystical Theology*, p. 211: he remarks that the
current view of the person – as 'a human subject over against whom
exists the range of objects for potential mastery or subordination' –
when applied to God, makes of God 'a particularly powerful and invis-
ible subject who acts over against human subjects, and must then
withdraw in order to permit their freedom to act autonomously (as
though God were one of the acting subjects of the world who only
happens to be more powerful than the others and so gets to be God
instead of some other possible candidate)'.

processes in such a way that our decisions are truly ours
AND truly what God desires in and through our own desiring. This model enables us to see how a person who seeks
God can 'do God's will' not just in the exercise of their
own initiative and responsibility, but also in and though the
very imperfections and limitations of human motives and
situation. Thus what is sought in the *Exercises* is 'God's
will for this particular person with this temperament and
character, with these gifts or limitations of nature and
grace, at this certain stage of development (physical, intellectual, emotional, moral, religious)'; thus understood it
'involves this person's relationship with God and with other
humans in this present situation with all its circumstances
of place, time, culture, social structures, customs and so
on.'[60] In other words, 'What appears in the abstract more
to the glory [of God] may not be so at all in the concrete'.[61]

Two caveats, however, should be noted with regard to
the collaboration model. It can be misleading to identify
'doing God's will' with making the best decision one can,
for such an identification can obscure the essential relational component of the process of finding God's will. In
the experience of doing God's will, God, for Ignatius,
never disappears behind a moral imperative. It can also be
misleading to identify the will of God with 'our own
deepest desires', unless the person making such a claim
understands that our own deepest *desires are those where
we experience the desires of the Spirit *within* our own
desires – and those are indeed both our deepest desires and
the most authentically our own.

Certitude

In situations where objective criteria are not determinative,
what importance does a spirituality of God's will attach to

---

[60] Jules Toner, *Discerning God's Will*, p. 26; he refers to the Annotations
      [Exx. 4, 9, 10, 14, 16, 18–20] and to two Notes [Exx. 162, 205].
[61] Ibid. p. 29.

certitude? Ignatius claims that there are situations when 'seeking' becomes 'finding', and even in default of coercive objective criteria, we can be assured of knowing the response, the 'yes', wished by God for us in a given situation or moment. Basic to Ignatius' spirituality is the conviction that God, who invites us to seek and do his will, can bring us to know without doubt, even in situations left to our own freedom of choice, the course of action by which we 'do God's will', do, that is to say, what is 'more pleasing' to God. Ignatius' own life furnishes many examples of such certitudes, e.g. his decision at Manresa to abandon abstinence from meat,[62] or his decision to resist the combined desire of the Pope and Holy Roman Emperor to have Francis Borgia made a cardinal.[63] Clarities of this kind arise out of the Three Times of Election, whether they occur during the *Exercises* themselves, or in the decisions of daily life. An indication of the status Ignatius accords to the subjective certitude arising out of discernment-based election is his insistence that in the *Exercises* themselves such a decision, even if 'mutable' should not be called in question unless clear reasons emerge for doing so (cf. [Exx. 173]).

On the question of certitude, it is important, however, to be clear on certain distinctions. First the certitude of discernment is that of a here-and-now *response of the will.* How our response will be eventually translated into *action,* and whether the future will work out as our response might lead us to anticipate, these do not fall within the certitudes proper to the discernment of God's will, certitudes which do not break into the mystery of God's mind or bring knowledge of the future. Hence, our subjective 'yes' does

---

[62] '... he [Ignatius] was incapable of being doubtful about this: rather he could not but make up his mind that he had to eat meat', *Personal Writings*, 'Reminiscences', §27, p. 25.

[63] 'If I did not act thus I would be (and am) quite certain in myself that I would not give good account of myself before God our Lord, rather a wholly bad one', *Personal Writings*, Letter 28 (5 June, 1552) [MHSI IV, 2652], pp. 245–6.

not guarantee that the situation or *state of life – *marriage, priesthood, membership of a religious order – to which we assent will necessarily materialize. Nevertheless, unless and until we are led to other responses, we are committed by the personally discerned perception of God's will at a given moment.

But although situations arise in which we can be sure of our subjective response, Ignatius does not portray the faithful Christian life as constantly doubt-free. To discern God's will requires freedom from the influence of disordered *affection, which in turn requires the freedom of *indifference, the positive *desire for God's universal will, a Christ-dominated outlook – and not many of our choices are made in this climate. But, these considerations apart, to imagine that life can ever be simply a doubt-free progress from one clarity to the next would greatly oversimplify the ways God involves himself in our human processes; and it is important to realize that the will of God is not only that which we can find and know; it is also that which we desire and seek – through often complex, obscure and extended processes. Hence, one of the ways we 'do' God's will is precisely in seeking it, and it is precisely in this sense that 'doing God's will' is always possible.

Part II
Terms of the *Exercises*

Agendo (or agere) contra

A recurrent theme of the *Exercises* is the principle of 'going against'[1] (generally known in its Latin form *agendo contra*) according to which temptations or disordered tendencies are best dealt with by 'diametrically opposed' action: 'when the person engaged in the spiritual life shows a bold front against those temptations and acts in a way diametrically opposed to them' [Exx. 325], and see [Exx. 16, 319]. If tempted to cut *prayer short, stay in prayer a little longer than intended; if drawn to a possession or office in a way that impedes freedom to seek God's will, ask in prayer for the very *poverty against which natural inclination recoils [Exx. 157].

It should be noted that in Ignatius' ordinary usage *agendo contra* refers not to the constant tensions of Christian existence as such (hence its use in the Kingdom exercise is not typical [Exx. 97]), but to specific here and now imbalances or disordered tendencies or attachments. Its purpose is to achieve balance and liberty of spirit, and to help to build habits. Thus Ignatius appeals to the *agendo contra* principle in order to bring a poorly attuned conscience to the mean between the coarse and the over-sensitive [Exx. 350] or to counter scrupulous misgivings about *vainglory [Exx. 351]. Measures are dropped or modified as their purpose is attained; in the course of healing, as Ignatius explained in a letter to his brother, 'when a serious wound has to be cured, first they use one sort of ointment, then another in the middle of the process, and finally another at the end'.[2]

Agendo contra is practised in a context of faith, and its effectiveness as a tool for spiritual progress – and the key to its practical application – lies in its relation to certain basic motifs of Ignatian spirituality. Hence it must always be practised as an act of collaboration with the action of the

---

[1] [Perhaps 'counter-attack' gives a better feel for this phrase.]
[2] Ignatius of Loyola, letter to Martín García de Oñaz, end of June 1532 (no. 3: MHSI ed., I, 77–83), *Personal Writings*, p. 119.

*Holy Spirit and never simply as a therapeutic or self-disciplinary tactic. To describe *agendo contra* as a process of the Spirit is to link it with spiritual *desire. For while consisting, in one respect, precisely in resisting desire, it draws its effectiveness from other desires, less impellingly felt, yet more truly our own.

Agere contra also requires the discerning self-awareness that is both the condition and the consequence of personal guidance by the Holy Spirit, a self-awareness that includes the knowledge of personal demons and of deeper personal issues behind the obvious and superficial phenomena. It should be noted in this connection that *agendo contra* is directed not only against temptation but against the tempter, 'the enemy', a figure conceived by Ignatius as a shrewd tactician: as imagined in the Meditation on the Two Standards, 'he orders them [the demons] to lay traps and chains, and he tells them that first they must tempt people to covet wealth ... so that they might come more readily to the empty honours of the world, and in the end to unbounded pride' [Exx. 142]. Going against the tempter may entail going against the ways in which the tempter works, often at the level of not immediately apparent weaknesses, fears or dependencies. For instance, if apparently 'proud' behaviour is covering up an inner lack of self-confidence, it may be the lack of self confidence rather than the 'proud' behaviour that needs to be gone against.[3] In the case of a person driven to apply *agendo contra* to endless trivialities, the appropriate object might well be the rigid attitude or its cause [Exx.350]. Discriminating use of the principle must also take account of 'times, persons and places'. This criterion may impose respect for the requirements of edification and of apostolic effectiveness – as Ignatius came to understand at Manresa when he abandoned the eccentricities of appearance that had served him well as an antidote to personal vanity, but which could only retard the emerging

---

[3]   In the letter to Sr Teresa Rejadell (18 June 1536) Ignatius counsels against false humility: *Personal Writings*, letter 4 (no. 7: I, 99–107), pp. 129–35.

apostolic effectiveness of his dealings with other people.[4]

Agendo contra is not, then, as simple a matter as it might sometimes appear to be. It is more than a practical aid to behaviour modification or habit building, of a kind that could equally operate outside of a faith context. And even when exercised in the context of faith, unreflective or undiscerning applications of the idea can negate and even reverse its effectiveness. It ranks however among the more important of Ignatius' practices as expressing commitment to growth in the Spirit and to the practical realism, and self-discipline that are the measure of sincerity on our side of the process. And it must never be forgotten that the deeper and more self-confrontational kinds of *agere contra*, such as that suggested in the context of the Meditation on the Three Classes [Exx. 157], are made by grace in God's time and are not an act of will to which one can force oneself or impose on others.[5]

Going against may be an external action (praying longer), or doing the very thing one is tempted not to do out of fear of vainglory; but it may be an interior action (praying to be chosen for the *poverty against which one naturally recoils); it may consist in opting for a *desire, a tendency, etc. The 'going against' texts represent, therefore, variations on a theme rather than applications of a uniform idea. Between them they show certain *characteristics of Ignatian outlook*. One opposes not only the temptation but the tempter, the personal 'enemy'; opposition to temptation contains an element analogous to a

---

[4] 'In Manresa itself, where he was for almost a year, once he began to be consoled by God and saw the fruit he was bringing forth in souls as he dealt with them, he left aside those eccentricities he had from before. Now he cut his nails and his hair regularly', *Personal Writings*, Reminiscences, §29, p. 26.

[5] [It is clear from the notes he added here that Ivens was drawing on the work of Edouard Pousset, *Life in Faith and Freedom*, translated and edited by Eugene L. Donahue, Anand-India, 1980 (originally published as *La vie dans la foi et la liberté: Essai sur les Exercices Spirituels de St. Ignace de Loyola*, Paris 1971); in particular p. 214.]

personal confrontation. But the enemy need not in every case correspond to an external agent. For Ignatius *going against* the tempter has two implications: (i) one opposes a power which is destructive if allowed its head, but weak if resisted; (ii) the 'right thing' is still the right thing even if self-interest contaminates my reasons for wanting to do it; and situations and persons can suffer because someone's personal need for *agere contra* takes precedence over a right course of action

Agendo contra appears in various forms, but basic to all of them is the principle that, while the main action of the Spirit is the positive action of bringing about our conversion and growth, a necessary correlative of this action is the elimination of whatever within ourselves blocks this work. Hence, while our own main cooperation is with the positive work of the Spirit, our co-operation requires conscious and deliberate collaboration in the mastering of the opposing forces.

Colloquy

Meditation, consideration and above all imaginative contemplation lead into the *prayer of colloquy. In numerous places the text of the *Exercises* specifies the nature, content and purpose of this prayer in some detail. But the first point to make is that 'colloquy' is a personal and spontaneous prayer, and never a set task to be performed on set lines. As a personal prayer it has the features of conversational exchange; it is a prayer therefore not simply of speaking but of listening. It is a prayer of the heart characterized by the quality of friendship or the familiarity of an ideal master-servant relationship. In the contemplations of the *Exercises* it is always in some sense an encounter between the exercitant in the situation and needs of the present moment of his/her personal history with Christ as he reveals himself through a moment of the history of his mortal life. Hence it will seek insight into the meaning of the mystery for the person praying and especially its bearing on the way God is calling him or her to conversion and service.

Much of the guidance offered by the text of the *Exercises* in connection with the colloquy serves simply to point up the inherent characteristics of a form of *prayer which in the *Exercises* almost makes itself, as the processing of the word develops through meditation or imaginative contemplation. Colloquy-prayer is not, however, left wholly to the spontaneity of the exercitant. At various points, the *Exercises* provide the colloquies with a definite and sometimes developed content, calculated to arouse desires and dispositions, directed (in the case of the Triple Colloquies quite explicitly) to conversion and *election.

Moreover, the *Exercises* insist on colloquy as the conclusion of prayer. In the course of an exercise, the prayer of colloquy might indeed arise spontaneously at any time, as several Directories point out;[6] but the *Exercises* themselves make no reference to colloquy except as the termination of a prayer. The phrases, 'end with a colloquy', 'make the Triple Colloquy' may be a little peremptory,[7] but they make their point unambiguously: every prayer in the *Exercises* culminates in colloquy, and colloquy is the note on which every prayer comes to an end.

These two features provide the key to the special impor-

---

6   *Directories* 'When distracted by a variety of thoughts, or oppressed by various spiritual desolations ... he should turn humbly upon himself and acknowledge his own wretchedness and worthlessness, making use of various colloquies either with his own soul or with God', Domenech (*Directories*, p. 74); cf. *Miró, de Fabi, 1599* (*Directories*, pp. 169, 193, 316).

7   [In an added note Ivens comments that the language of Ignatius is said to seem 'stilted' at times.]

tance of colloquy in the *Exercises:* it is the function of
colloquy to carry prayer forward into the future, with its
inseparable tasks of ongoing personal conversion and
seeking God's will in the building of his kingdom. The
significance of the concluding colloquy prayer in the *Exercises* must be interpreted in relation to the meaning of
'contemplation' in the *Exercises.* This meaning is significantly different from that in Guigo's *Ladder.*[8] Here *oratio*
(the prayer of the heart to 'drive away evil and obtain what
is good'), though clearly corresponding in many respects to
the Ignatian colloquy, is the third stage in a sequence which
reaches its completion in a contemplation conceived as
world-transcending, ecstatic, silent, unitive. That Ignatius
should see colloquy not as the preliminary to contemplation
but as its completion is explained by his understanding of
contemplation as consisting rather in an attention to Christ's
self-revelation in the 'mysteries' of the Gospel, not an end
in itself but having as its objective the seeking and finding
God's will in love-inspired discipleship.[9]

---

[8] Guigo II (+ *c.*1188), prior of La Grande Chartreuse and author of the
    Ladder of Monks, is an important figure in the genealogy of the Ignat-
    ian *Exercises.* The significance of Guigo's book consists mainly in his
    analysis of *lectio divina* into a four-stage process made up of reading,
    meditation, prayer (*oratio* in Latin), and contemplation. As the author
    explains:
       Reading is the careful study of the scripture, concentrating all one's
       powers on it. *Meditation* is the busy application of the mind to seek
       with the help of one's reason for knowledge of hidden truth. *Prayer*
       is the heart's devoted turning to God in order to repulse evil and
       obtain what is good. *Contemplation* is when the mind is in some sort
       lifted up to God and held above itself, so that it tastes the joys of
       everlasting sweetness. *Scala claustralium* [= *Letter on the Interior
       Life,* publ. in *The Way* (1965), p. 334].
    This division was taken up into the spiritual doctrine of García Ximenes
    de Cisneros, abbot of Montserrat, which in turn was undoubtedly the
    channel through which it came to the knowledge of Ignatius. The echoes
    of Guigo in the *Exercises* are in many ways obvious, but Ignatius also
    departs from Guigo in the order in which he places contemplation and
    oratio, clearly the equivalent of the Ignatian colloquy. [Cf. Javier
    Melloni, SJ, *The Exercises of St Ignatius Loyola in the Western Tradi-
    tion,* Leominster 2000, pp. 24–25, 28–9.]
[9] [Exx. 104].

The Triple Colloquy

Among the concluding prayers of colloquy [Exx. 147, 156], the *Exercises* attach particular significance to 'the three colloquies' (called in the Vulgate,[10] the 'triple colloquy' [Exx. 168]). The importance and effectiveness of this prayer can be accounted for in various ways.

(i) It is a consciously Trinitarian prayer, leading to the Father through the incarnate Word, son of Mary.

(ii) The sequence, Mary – Jesus – the Father, re-traces the movement of salvation history: from the *fiat* of Mary, to the coming of Christ into the world, to reconciliation with the Father.

(iii) As a form of petitionary prayer, the progression through three separate colloquies and the ascending levels of accompaniment bring home the fact that in both the First and Second Week the *graces asked for are truly gifts, beyond our capacity to bring about ourselves, and indeed not lightly to be asked for.

(iv) But the three prayers are not only petitions; they are 'colloquies', as Ignatius understands the term: personal, conversation-like modes of prayer in which understanding can develop and feelings can be processed.

(v) In both Weeks the first two colloquies, those with Mary and with Jesus, will make the exercitant aware of the lives of Mary and Jesus that bear particularly on the graces being asked for.

Contempt

One of the more challenging features of the *Exercises* is their insistence that in order to follow the way of radical

---

[10] [The officially approved Latin version.]

discipleship, one must set a positive value on, indeed pray to experience, situations described by the words 'abuse' [Exx. 98], 'insults' [Exx. 98, 147], 'contempt' [Exx. 146], 'humiliations' [Exx. 147, 167]. These translate a still wider range of vocabulary in the Spanish and Latin texts; and their vigour makes us aware how far Ignatius believed that graced *desire in this matter could extend. But their meaning must not be confined to experiences of an extreme or dramatic kind. Essentially, Ignatius is identifying a particular kind of *poverty, impossible perhaps to epitomise in a single word, but readily explained by the antitheses of the Two Standards meditation. As the enemy leads people into *pride by way of worldly fame, so Christ leads to *humility by way of whatever is antithetical to fame, broadly rather than narrowly understood: failure, experiences of diminishment, neglect or disparagement – all situations of this kind are included under this wider category of poverty.

Touching deeper levels of the person, situations of 'contempt' are regarded by Ignatius as more immediately challenging than material poverty, and if accepted in faith, as more immediately proximate to humility. Thus in the offering of the Kingdom [Exx. 98] 'outrage' and 'contempt' precede actual and spiritual poverty; and the famous elaboration of the Third Mode of Humility in the *Constitutions*, is concerned totally with *desire for the opposite of 'honours, fame and the esteem for a great name on earth', with no reference to material poverty at all.[11]

All this said, it must be added emphatically that humiliating situations are spiritually significant only to the extent to which they have faith-meaning. In matters where we can choose to incur or avoid such situations, choice must

---

[11] '... where there would be no offense to his Divine Majesty ... they would wish to suffer injuries, false accusations, and affronts, and to be held and esteemed as fools ...' *General Examen of Candidates*, ch. 4, §44 (tr., Ganss, p. 108).

always be made in reference to the glory of God discerned within a positive outlook on *creation and a sense of the complexity of human reality.

Election

Election (the ordinary Spanish word for 'choice') is used in the *Exercises* to designate a choice marked by certain clear characteristics. First, the matter involves the quality of a person's *service of God, hence the question of the greater *glory. The presenting alternatives are both legitimate in themselves, hence belong to the space between the obligatory and the forbidden (cf. [Exx. 23]). There is no objectively right thing to do. General norms must certainly be taken into account (the word of God in scripture and tradition, objective morality, acts of authority, specific commitments and responsibilities, etc.), but in themselves the application of such norms cannot be decisive and the issue in the end must be resolved on the level of personal intuition and judgement. It is the implicit contention of the *Exercises* that in choices of this kind it is possible to find, on the subjective basis of discerning intuition and judgement, the *here-and-now* response that God asks us to make.

To avoid oversimplification it should be added that in order to emphasize the particular significance of major (and especially life-changing) decisions, Ignatius in the *Exercises* distinguishes between election in the full sense, and the more everyday decisions of reform within a *state of life: 'instead of an election they can very profitably be given a framework and method by which to amend and reform themselves in their personal lives and states' [Exx. 189].[12]

The *Exercises* contain a doctrine and procedure in relation to elections in the full sense in which three elements can be broadly distinguished:

   (i) there is the insistence on the preliminary dispositions necessary if these decisions are to be approached as involving the search and assent to God's will: *indifference, positive *desire for God's will whatever it might prove to be; knowledge of Christ through the Gospel; openness to all the objective ways in which that will is mediated to us;

  (ii) there is a form of *prayer which expressly looks to a culmination not within itself, but beyond itself in a process of search for and ultimate assent to God's will outside itself;

 (iii) the decision is on the basis of the three kinds of *experiential evidence* of God's will set out under the head of the Three Times of Election.

The key to the often protracted and complex processes, through which one finds God's will concretely for oneself, is to be found in the three kinds of action of the *Holy Spirit, or of Spirit-given evidence: the unmistakable call; tested consolation; Spirit-enlightened reason together with, where necessary, the use of imagination to check the quality of emerging desires or reactions. Of these ways, it should be noted that all three are in a sense 'obediential': obedience in the case of the second being to tested *consolation (as distinct from the voice of desolation or the bad spirit masquerading under the appearance of the good); and in the case of the third to 'reason' as distinct from sensuality. All three ways moreover require the setting aside of 'self-love, self-will and self-interest'.

It must be remembered that in the context of the *Exercises* the exercitants are concerned with discerning God's

---

[12] On the practical significance of this distinction see *Understanding*, pp. 129–130, 144.

will for themselves, *here and now*; this may not always be possible, but there are situations, Ignatius believed, when we can indeed be assured and confident of finding the response, the 'yes' that God asks us to make.

In the text of the *Exercises* election is central and integral, but this does not mean that an election in the full sense has to be made in the course of the Exercises before a person can claim truly to have made the *Exercises* of Ignatius. While one must reject the once common view that election is in practice something of a rare event in the *Exercises*, it is also important to keep in mind the principles and practice of Ignatius himself, who disallowed election of a state in life in the case of Jesuit novices[13] (assumed to have made such an election already) and more generally showed considerable caution as to who might be considered suitable for election. But the significance of election in the *Exercises* is not confined to that of any particular election that an exercitant might make, but rather in its implicit understanding of the *will of God and the implications of this understanding for daily life. Implicit in the *Exercises* is the assumption that God's will can be personal, that within the constants of the moral and Christian life there is a will of God for the individual, which it is therefore possible for the individual to 'find' – a unique way which is the Spirit-guided working out of each one's personal *vocation. It is a position which, though implicit in Catholic orthodoxy, has tended widely to be played down in practice. One of the effects of highlighting it – as the *Exercises* do – is to give new significance to a whole range of choices once regarded as essentially distracting, inconsistent with contemplation,

13 'Concerning our own members, there is no objection to giving them the *Exercises* of the other weeks also [not just the First Week], but without entering with these men upon the matter of the election of a state of life, although the method which is taught in the *Exercises* could be applied to other choices, without touching on the state of life', *Epistolae S. Ignatii* [MHSI], XII, 141; the original is in Italian and comes in a letter written by Polanco at Ignatius' request, 4 July, 1556, shortly before his death; cf. de Guibert, pp. 124–5.

best avoided if possible. Where the concept of God's will
for the individual is to the fore, many such decisions,
including many which are inseparable from apostolic life,
are seen to have the quality of 'election', as the term is
understood in the *Exercises*, choices requiring a contemplative process and a union precisely in order to be made.
    All this said, it is important not to play down other ways of
perceiving and deciding for God's will. To recognize and
decide – for what is objectively right and against what is
objectively wrong – may require the mentally clarifying First
Week discernment rules, but not the more advanced discernment of the Second. However, this does not imply a distinction between inferior and superior in the quality of the human
act. Concretely to meet the commitment of the First Kind of
Humility ('even if I were made lord of all . . . I would not . . .
set about breaking any law . . . which obliges me under pain
of mortal sin' [Exx. 165]) may demand profound renuncia-
tion of self-love, self-will and self-interest. Moreover it
should be noted that with regard to the Decalogue, the capital
sins, etc., the *Exercises* are not content simply with an obedience of execution and will, but invite the exercitant to
contemplative insight into the inner meaning of these.
    It is also important to recognize that one of the most impor-
tant ways in which a human being does the will of God is in
acts of free *acceptance* of situations where no external choice
is possible, acceptance of given limitations and diminish-
ments. While it is especially important for an apostolic spirituality to eschew attitudes of fatalism or inappropriate
passivity, an authentic spirituality of God's will requires a
recognition that the supreme moments of human freedom
consist precisely in acts of acceptance – ultimately the acceptance of one's own death. There are times when passivity is
chosen as a possible alternative to action. To decide for inaction against possible action, for letting something happen as
distinct from making something happen – this is one of the
choices that may fall under the category of election. But there
is another and more radical option for passivity, namely the
free decision for acceptance, in the face of a situation impos-

sible in itself to change – such an act of freedom occurs in the acceptance from God's hand of one's own death.[14]

Enemy of human nature

The words 'devil' and 'Satan' do not occur in the *Exercises*, which refer instead to 'Lucifer', the 'bad spirit', the 'bad angel',[15] and, most commonly to the 'enemy',[16] with its important variant, 'enemy of our human nature'.[17] The frequent use of 'enemy' testifies to a quality which, even if easily caricatured, is characteristic of Ignatius' outlook: his sense that we live in a situation of spiritual conflict, contending with an opponent, who is described in the *Exercises* as the enemy not of Christ but of ourselves.

In our conflict with the 'enemy of human nature', what is ultimately at issue is eternal salvation. However, but the phrase draws attention to the here-and-now and to the whole person, and evokes especially the inner turmoil and the unfreedom of one led by the Evil One against the peace and integrity of lives given to Christ, as suggested by the contrast between the opposed leaders in the Two Standards meditation [Exx. 136–146].

14 [These lines gain an added poignancy when one realizes that Ivens wrote them while preparing for his own imminent death.]
15 Mention of Lucifer in the Two Standards [Exx. 136–138], of the 'bad angel' in the Rules for Discernment [Exx. 331–332]; 'bad spirit(s)' are much more common [Exx. 4, 6, 8, 9, 17, 176, 177, 315, 328 333, 335, 336].
16 Some eighteen references to the 'enemy', and another five to the 'enemies' (plural).
17 Eight references to the 'enemy of human nature' [Exx. 7, 10, 135, 136, 325, 326, 327, 334].

Only in the Two Standards does Ignatius depict the devil as
a figure of dread. In the *Exercises* he is essentially an
omnipresent malign intelligence, which operates through
plausibility and deceit: hence the importance of Lucifer, the
fallen angel of light. To resist, and eventually overthrow, the
'enemy' it is therefore necessary to become aware of these
deceits. This perspective gives the *Exercises* an essentially
robust and practical attitude which must not degenerate on the
one hand into anxiety or on the other into complacency.

Examen

Though not to be found in the English dictionary, the word
examen is preferred to the term 'examination of conscience'
to designate a way of prayer considered by Ignatius an integral and indispensable element in all daily prayer. As set
out in the *Exercises*, its two forms, the particular and the
general [Exx. 24–43], witness in various ways to the practical realism of Ignatius, especially in reducing more
diffuse traditional practices to simple methods, and in
recognizing that in the realm of spiritual development, one
cannot concentrate on everything at once. An insistence on
the concrete and specific is characteristic of the *examen*;
but it would be a misunderstanding of it, and especially of
its place in maturing lives, to see it only as an ascetical
application of moral norms to behaviour.
    Its deep significance lies in three related characteristics. Its
context is the contemplative vision of reality sought in the
Contemplatio ad amorem [Exx. 234]. It is a *prayer of
discerning reflection, in which one becomes aware of the
movements of the spirits on one's life and of one's responses

to them. It is a means of discerning the continuing call to
*service in and through the events and situations of life.

While the two *examens*, particular and general, are
specific exercises done – ordinarily together – at set times, to
avail oneself of them according to Ignatius' mind they need
also to constitute a reflective thread running through the day.

Graces: First Week and beyond

In the text the First Week graces fall under eight general
heads, which together form a certain dynamic sequence.
Four of these graces are *petitioned* (P); the others are
presented as the ordinary *consequences* (C) of receiving one
of these petitioned graces. These further graces are mainly
specified in connection with the *colloquy. It should be
noted that in four places the grace is associated with a reso-
lution or *decision* (D).

The graces are as follows:

(i) (P) 'personal shame and *confusion' [Exx. 48];
(ii) (C + D) the grace of a *prayer before the *Cross against
the background of the triple sin leading into the question,
'What have I done for Christ?', etc. [Exx. 53];
(iii) (P) 'mounting and intense sorrow, and tears' [Exx. 55];
(iv) (C) 'an exclamation of wonder' (this is more than just a
point,[18] but rather a beginning of the colloquy)[Exx. 60];
(v) (C + D) thanksgiving for mercy leading to a decision 'to

---

[18] [The word 'point' is traditionally used to indicate one of various items
for reflection in a meditation: thus the New Testament Materials for
Contemplation [Exx. 261–312] are divided in this way; cf. *Prayer
(methods of).]

amend my life' (note that in the Vulgate version of this
colloquy not only are thanks given for the 'mercy',
gratias agendo, but the notion of 'extolling' that mercy,
extollendo, is added) [Exx. 61];

(vi) (P + D) 'inner knowledge of my sins and an *abhorrence
for them'; also, 'that I may feel the disorder in my
actions' and have 'knowledge of the world' leading thus
to decisions 'to amend my life' and 'cut myself off from
worldly things and vanities' [Exx. 63];

(vii) (P) *fear based on 'an interior sense of the suffering
undergone by the damned' [Exx. 65];

(viii)(C) thanksgiving (again) for the kindness and mercy of
God [Exx. 71].

The petitioned graces are those Ignatius thinks it proper to
ask for and systematically to seek in *prayer. But if these are
given, he seems to assume that further graces, associated
with the colloquies, will follow. The exercitant
should expect these and be open to them. But they can in no
way be induced and their position, precisely as further
graces, seems to imply that to try to induce them, or even to
ask for them before one has received the more basic graces,
would have been seen by Ignatius as bypassing the process.

One might sum up by saying that there are many interconnected First Week graces, of which two can be singled
out as nodal points giving the week its distinctive shape:
the grace of contrition and the grace of wonder/thanks-
giving/praise. Of these, Ignatius refers to the first twice
[Exx. 4 and 89] in summarizing the 'what I want' of the
Week. Note also that the Directory dictated to Fr Juan
Alfonso de Vitoria indicates that 'if the exercitant is a spiritual person who has already lamented [literally "wept
over" *llorado*] his sins', the First Week might be given
'in a very short time'.[19] Ignatius envisages that an exercitant might already have received the grace described,[20] but

---

[19] *Directories*, p. 22; Ignatius is thought to have dictated the *Directory* to
this Spanish Jesuit in 1555.
[20] [Exx. 4, 55, 89].

he clearly held that such a grace was an essential stage in the process of spiritual maturation. Hence the purpose of the First Week is to bring people to this stage, if they have not reached it already, and, if they have, to return to it, even if briefly.

However, justice to the First Week requires emphasis also on the grace of wonder and thanksgiving which concludes both the second and the fifth exercises, and is perhaps implicit in the colloquy of the *Cross [Exx. 53]. 'Contrition' and 'wonder' must therefore be understood in relation to one another. Contrition alone does not represent the fullness of the First Week grace; it must be completed by thanksgiving and wonder. On the other hand, the grace of the First Week is not an isolated experience of thanksgiving and wonder with no base in the experience of contrition. The full First Week grace also includes the graces of the Triple *Colloquy.

Finally, two general features of the First Week seem relevant to understanding its distinctive graces: first, the emphatically *personal* dimension of the various graces (the Creator dies 'for my sins' [Exx. 53], mounting and intense sorrow for 'my sins' [Exx. 55], etc.), even if exclusive individualism is certainly not to be read into this feature; second, the reach into *decision*, the movement from the 'affective' response to the 'effective' response, by which, in a sense, the former is authenticated.

Beyond the First Week

In the *Exercises* desires are set out in a developmental order, *desire leading to desire as *graces* are progressively 'found' in a sequence in which the more fundamental desires and graces give way to those of a finer and more mature quality. The sequence can be summarized as follows:

1. Desire for the graces of conversion: *confusion, contrition, the *fear that leads to gratitude, together with the graced

aversion for sin (*abhorrence, *aborrecimiento*) that is the
corollary of converted desire (First Week).
2. Desire to share the desires of Christ himself for the world
and to hear his call to *service (Kingdom). From the standpoint of the Ignatian doctrine on *desire, the Kingdom
exercise [Exx. 91-98] has a double interest: it introduces a
desire which, however formulated, will always be at the
centre of Ignatian spirituality; and it illustrates the subtlety
of Ignatius' step-by-step pedagogy of desire – how he sets
out to arouse a response, capturing the exercitant by a
general vision, while at the same time finishing with an
offering which for the moment the exercitant is asked only
to consider, not to make his or her own.
3. Desires for the graces that constitute a progressive deepening and intensification of the exercitant's relationship with
Christ; such desires to know and love lead in the Third and
Fourth Weeks to desires for closer union, a share in the
suffering of the passion and the joy of the resurrection.
4. Desire for *poverty: the Second Week is founded on the
premise that as the exercitant grows in knowledge and love
of Christ and the sense of discipleship, there will arise, incip-
iently in the Kingdom exercise, explicitly in the Two Standards meditation, a desire for poverty, not only for spiritual
poverty but also for the situation of actual poverty.[21] Essentially, a situation is one of actual poverty to the extent to
which it is antithetical to the *riches and worldly honour
which are the objects of cupidity, but is a situation assumed
by Ignatius to be instinctively and socially undesirable. To be
'poor in spirit' a situation of actual poverty is not essential,
but there can be no poverty of spirit except where such a situation is, at some deep level of the self, experienced as desirable. Thus the central grace of the Second Week is one by
which a situation – one without meaning and value *without
Christ* – acquires meaning and becomes desirable, even
something one might ask for, when perceived in its relationship to one's growth in the love and imitation of Christ, and
in the promotion of Christ's kingdom.
5. Desire to find God in *all things.

---

[21] For ways of interpreting 'actual poverty', not confined to the material
sense, see *poverty.

History

A term used in the *Exercises* with a certain flexibility.
Primarily it refers to the contents of the Gospel texts. But
it is also used of the imaginative constructs proposed for
the contemplation on the Incarnation [Exx. 102] and the
meditation on the Two Standards [Exx. 137], while in the
Three Classes the 'history' is a parable about human attitudes [Exx. 150].

Whether or not the 'history' is true in the literal sense
in which Ignatius would have applied the concept of
history to the Gospels, it always serves to give to *prayer
a foundation in some objective reality. His practice of
beginning the various exercises with 'histories' also testifies to Ignatius' preference for a concrete approach over
an abstract one.

'I shall look upon and contemplate our Lady and the infant
Jesus; and as though present, serve them in their needs with all
possible homage and reverence.' *First point, Meditation on the
Nativity* [Exx. 114].

Lectio divina

This Latin expression originates from the monastic spirituality of the High Middle Ages, and stands for the attentive *reading* of Scripture as the first stage of a sequence by which the assimilation of the word of God, through meditation and *prayer (*oratio*) leads to contemplation.

The importance of this reading and the nature of its relationship to the second step, meditation, is expressed in various ways, e.g. by 'reading' one takes in the nourishment, which 'meditation' then digests; 'reading' stakes out the site of a treasure, which 'meditation' digs out, etc.[22]

In the *Exercises* this four-stage process is taken over by Ignatius with significant variations in the method of prayer of the Four Weeks. The importance of the first step, reading, is reflected in his insistence that meditation and contemplation be built on the word of God, the 'true historical foundation', in the circumstances of the time. In the *Exercises*, however, access to this foundation comes from the director whose task it is to recount the gospel story accurately, and only with such commentary or explanation as might be necessary. In the *Exercises* this substitute for personal reading is to be explained partly by the circumstances of the time, partly by the nature of the *Exercises*. Today no one would see the director's exposition as excluding personal reading, though in the context of the *Exercises* this reading will be made with the points of the director or of the *Exercises* as key.

For Scripture-based prayer outside the *Exercises* it is important to remember that the first step, *lectio divina*, reading of the text in the consciousness precisely of preparing for *prayer, is integral to the process. In such reading one is alert for particular details – words, persons, acts – which seem personally significant here and now. In this context the text might be described as the '*words*' of God which one reads in order to find the ways in which, at this

---

[22] See under *Colloquy the note on Guigo II, the Carthusian.

particular moment, through these, the Living *Word* seems to invite response in prayer.

Petition

In the *Exercises*, petitionary *prayer is concerned with personal conversion and growth in Christ, with life-situations entailed by the following of Christ, and with seeking the *will of God in choices. It is characterised by two overlapping distinctions. There is a distinction between spontaneous petition (cf [Exx. 54, 109, 199]), including prayer made in relation to the *materia subjecta*, the 'proposed material' or 'matter under consideration' (e.g. [Exx. 4, 49, 74, 204, 225]), and what can be termed the 'given' petitions (preliminary prayer, petitionary preludes, certain of the colloquy petitions). And within the 'given petitions' there is a distinction between those made unconditionally, on the grounds that God certainly wishes the petitioner to have the *grace asked for (e.g. the highest spiritual poverty) and petitions made with the condition that the thing petitioned be for God's *glory, or according to his will. (e.g. actual *poverty or opprobrium). It should further be noted that the given petitions are crucial to the dynamic of the *Exercises* not only singly but as a sequence, in which as graces 'sought' are progressively 'found', one petition will lead to another in a series of ascending steps.

Why is petition central to the *Exercises*? On what basis can Ignatius assume that a series of pre-determined petitions will always correspond to an exercitant's needs and desires? How far, if at all, do the petitionary provisions of the *Exercises* make concessions to the individual? The

answers to these questions are to be found in the nature of
desire and its place in the life in the Spirit. A person open
to the Spirit experiences desires which are both their own
and those of the indwelling *Holy Spirit, who leads us
forward through such desires on the road of conversion and
*service. By expressing these desires in petitionary prayer,
we own them, commit ourselves to them, and thus freely
collaborate in the Spirit's processes. In particular, an
earnest and repeated (but not forced) prayer of petition is
one of the more effective ways in which desire is moved
forward from the incipient and fragile 'desire for the desire'
to intense commitment.[23]

The object of these desires may consist in some quite
specific gift or call that God wishes to make in our regard
(cf. [Exx. 199]). Other desires, however, belong to Christian faith as such and to the internal logic of all conversion
and all faith-maturation. Such are the desires articulated in
the 'given' petitions of the *Exercises*, including the 'conditional' petitions [Exx. 98, 146]; even in connection with
these Ignatius considers that the *desire* itself is a grace
proper to a mature Christian faith.

Does this mean that in the case of an ideally disposed
exercitant a steady progress through the desires of the *Exercises* will never be complicated by personal factors? While
exercitants frequently move with ease, almost naturalness,
through the sequence of named desires, nevertheless even
with an exercitant in the best of dispositions, the sequence
will not always coincide absolutely accurately with the
exercitant's own progress or even with his or her experience or way of articulating things. Often the block is simply
one of language. But the petitions may also have the effect
of confronting an exercitant with his or her own affective
divisions. That a desire is of the Spirit, and hence truly and
deeply our own, does not necessarily imply that the exerci-

---

[23] A candidate for the Society who 'does not experience in himself such
ardent desires in our Lord' should be asked 'whether he has any desires
to experience them', *General Examen of Candidates*, ch. 4, §102 (tr.,
Ganss, pp. 108–9); but see also [Exx. 155, 157, 168, 180].

tant will be immediately 'in touch' with such a desire, or
willing to acknowledge its presence within conflicting but
more imperiously felt desires of instinct. Petitionary prayer
in the *Exercises* may therefore be a complex co-operation
with the way God himself is at work in the dynamics of our
desires. Thus, amid conflicting desires petition may serve
to affirm which has our commitment; indeed precisely by
our prayer of petition we may be made to confront the force
of opposition between our deeper and our more imperiously
felt desire – as when the exercitant makes a prayer that puts
her in manifest opposition to carnal and worldly love [Exx.
98] or asks on his or her side for a situation against which
nature rebels [Exx. 157].

The wider reach of petitionary prayer

While the quality of petitionary prayer that is characteristic
of the *Exercises* – prayer to know God's will or to receive
some particular *grace – belongs also to the everyday
prayer of a person sincerely in search of God, the range of
petitionary prayer as a general practice is considerably
wider than this. The immediate motive of much everyday
petitionary prayer is to bring to God some desire or need
of our own, one perceived certainly as not manifestly
against God's will, but brought into prayer precisely as a
desire of ours, in the hope that in his goodness God will
grant what we ask.

   Petition of this kind can be made at all levels of prayer
from the highest to the most ambiguous. It is a mistake to
depreciate such prayer on the grounds that if God's will in
a particular matter is not certainly known, one should make
only the simple *fiat*, 'thy will be done'. For often it is the
will of God, who personally cares for us and has regard for
our desires, that we come before him precisely with our
own desires and needs, with the trust, humility and faith-
risk exemplified in the Gospels by the centurion (Luke 7:7),
the Canaanite woman (Matthew 15:22), blind Bartimaeus
(Mark 10:46–52), and many others who prayed earnestly to

Christ for themselves or for others. But prayer for favours
can also come out of egocentric or self protective or manip-
ulative motives, or rest on questionable assumptions
regarding God's will (e.g. that in war God is on the side of
the person praying).

In approaching a form of prayer capable of including this
range of quality two considerations in particular must be
kept in view. First, petitionary prayer presumes of its
nature a moment in which search for the divine will and the
acknowledgment of human need intersect; and second, it
can be a way in which we experience how our needs before
God change, as petitionary prayer develops with the growth
of a maturing faith-outlook and with increasing docility to
the teaching and guidance of the *Holy Spirit. Questions
about petitionary prayer can be answered only by following
the Spirit against a background of self-knowledge and
informed faith-outlook. But essentially in our petitionary
prayer it must be the Spirit who teaches us what to ask for
and how to pray; and it should always be part of our petitionary prayer not only to seek the guidance of the Spirit in
our here-and-now concern, but implicitly or explicitly to
pray that this moment of prayer be part of a Spirit-guided
process by which, through petitionary prayer itself, our
prayer becomes ever more authentic and mature.

Prayer

The *Exercises* include various kind of prayer ('prayer'
being understood in the broadest sense of the term). In the
Four Weeks the main form of prayer is 'imaginative
contemplation', with the occasional prayer of 'meditation',

and exercises which are best classified as 'considerations'. Added to the Four Weeks there is the Contemplation to attain love [Exx. 230–237], and the Three Ways of Praying [Exx. 238–260]. The categories of contemplation and meditation contain more specific ways of prayer within themselves, e.g., *colloquy, 'repetition', 'prayer of the senses'. And among the more important prayers of the *Exercises* there is the *examen.

Since a person making the *Exercises* spends up to five hours a day praying in these various ways, it is easy to think that the main purpose of the *Exercises* is to provide a school in prayer, and from this to conclude that there is a distinctive approach to prayer which can be called 'Ignatian', and that it will be a mark of a follower of Ignatian spirituality to pray habitually according to the general lines set down in the *Exercises*.

How far are these assumptions justified? Obviously there is a sense in which the *Exercises* are indeed a school for prayer. They introduce traditional approaches to prayer in a simple way that helps people to make their own prayer, and they teach the exercitant to deepen his or her prayer by reflecting on their experience of praying. Those who have made the *Exercises* will be likely to continue to avail themselves of their practical teaching on prayer in many ways: one form of prayer taught in the *Exercises*, the *examen*, will certainly pass from the *Exercises* into the realm of daily habit. Yet it can be misleading to describe the *Exercises* as a school for prayer. For prayer in the *Exercises* is a means to an end, and the end of the *Exercises* is a gospel-inspired conversion of mind and will together with a decision made in the context of such a conversion. The contemplations and meditations of the *Exercises*, and all the aids to prayer they provide, are selected and proposed in order to meet the particular end of the *Exercises*, not in order to propose a systematic doctrine on prayer, or to give the exercitant a prayer experience, though of course, they do this. Only when this is understood can the *Exercises* be described as a school for prayer.

The important and frequently neglected implication of
this is that the ways of prayer in the *Exercises* do not
constitute 'Ignatian prayer' in the sense that other kinds of
prayer are not Ignatian, or that the *Exercises* are designed
to provide permanent ways of praying. Such attitudes are
far removed from the open and flexible principles adopted
by Ignatius and the early Jesuits in spiritual direction: for
example, if a person appeared to be led in prayer by the
good spirit, then such a person should be left alone. The
fundamental norm for the rightness of any way of prayer
for an individual was whether through it God seemed most
to communicate himself; one of the clearest signs of a
suspect spirit in prayer was not departure from a set way,
but rather the failure of a person's prayer to confirm them
in their calling (in the case of Jesuits, to apostolic service).
In regard to the exercitant's subsequent life there is the
principle laid down for Francis Borgia:

> You should always take care to maintain your soul in peace,
> in quiet, and in readiness for whatever Our Lord might wish
> to do within it. There is no doubt that it is a greater virtue in
> the soul, and a greater grace, for it to be able to relish its Lord
> in a variety of duties and in a variety of places, rather than
> simply in one.[24]

Methods of prayer

'Imaginative contemplation': by contemplating the Gospels
imaginatively you enter into the Church's faith-memory of
Jesus, and his saving words and actions. You do this by
allowing the Gospel narrative to draw you inside itself so
that you become present to the event, involved in it, (much
as through memory and imagination you can re-live an
event of your own past). Your contemplation must be based
on the text, the word of God, but you must give imagination the freedom it needs to make your prayer of this event

---

[24] 'Letter to Francis Borgia' (MHSI *Epistolae Sti Ignatii*, No. 466, vol.
2, pp. 233–237; tr., *Personal Writings* (Letter 21), p. 205.

a personal experience, a real personal encounter between yourself and Jesus and the other participants in the scene. The Gospel narratives confine themselves to essentials and leave it to the imagination of the reader to fill them out. The elements of Ignatius' method can be summarized as follows:

(i) reading the text: shortly before you begin, make a careful reading of the Gospel narrative, noticing points that particularly strike you. Get the overall sequence into your mind and, especially if the narrative is long, break it down into heads (or 'points'). This reading corresponds to the ancient practice of *lectio divina*, and hence it should be made prayerfully, not just as a study;

(ii) entry: even in the prayerful general climate of a retreat, one does not pray all the time in the same way as during a set 'time of prayer' with its definite beginning, duration and end. The transition into the time of prayer is marked by some mental act. Ignatius suggests that 'for the space of an Our Father and, with my mind raised up, I consider how God our Lord is looking at me' [Exx. 75];

(iii) the preparatory prayer: 'I ask God our Lord for grace that all my intentions, actions and operations may be directed purely to the service and praise of his Divine Majesty' [Exx. 46]; Ignatius makes explicit mention of this prayer of *petition* every time he expounds a meditation or contemplation during the Four Weeks and he insists that it must never be changed [Exx. 49, 105], whatever may be the subject of prayer, and whatever more specific petitions one may wish to make. The overall sense is clear – the exercitant asks through grace to live ever more closely to the never to be fully attained ideal of an existence totally dedicated to the praise and *service of God;[25]

[25] However, there seems to have been some unclarity about the precise difference between 'actions' and 'operations'. In the Latin versions the distinction disappears: the Vulgate gives *vires et operationes* ('powers and operations'), and the Versio Prima has *intentiones et actiones*. Various interpretations are offered by modern commentators; the most practically useful distinction is between 'action' signifying the (inner) act (of decision), and 'operation' as its subsequent execution.

(iv) three preliminaries, or 'preludes':
  (1) the *history – recall the broad sequence of the passage you are about to contemplate; bring home to yourself that this incident is part of the unfolding drama of salvation history;
  (2) 'seeing the place' – the actions of Jesus, like ours, come about in a place – a house, a lakeside, a synagogue, a stretch of road – and the environment in which the event is enacted is an integral part of the event itself, and hence before contemplating the event, one imaginatively puts oneself into this place or places; in the *Exercises* Ignatius gives a few illustrations of imagined places: e.g. 'the synagogues, towns and villages[26] where Christ our Lord went preaching' [Exx. 91], 'the road from Nazareth to Bethlehem ... the length and breadth of it, whether it is a flat road or goes through valleys or over hills ... the place or grotto of the nativity ... how big or small it is, how high and what is in it' [Exx. 112]; seeing the place in this way also serves as an aid to 'centring', by using the imagination to bring the body to where the mind is;
  (3) '*petition': one names some particular gift or grace that one feels moved to ask for (compare the 'what are you looking for?' of John 1:38). The fundamental petition of every Christian who contemplates the Gospel is summed up by St Richard of Chichester: 'Three things I pray, to know you more clearly, to love you more dearly, to follow you more nearly'. But according to the subject of the text or your own needs, you may want to specify this in more particular ways.
(v) 'points': this is the body of the prayer, the actual contemplation to which the above practices are preparatory; make use of the breakdown of the material you have made in your preliminary reading. In contemplating a

---

[26] [As Ivens noted in the Introduction to his translation of the *Exercises* (2004), p. xi, the Spanish word translated 'villages' is *castillos* (hence the translation 'castles' adopted by him earlier in *Understanding* (1998), p. 80).]

longer incident, go through the sequence step by step, but at each step taking care to see 'the persons', listen to 'what they are saying', watch 'what they are doing' (e.g. [Exx. 114–116]). In the contemplation of a shorter or simpler text the step-by-step procedure may not be necessary, and it is enough to be present to the persons, words and actions that make up the total event. 'Persons, words, actions' are the key to Gospel contemplation; attention to them keeps the prayer open to the deeper meaning of the text, and serves as a natural defence against any tendency to make Gospel contemplation a study rather than prayer; 'persons, words actions' will ordinarily be three constantly shifting points of attention in the contemplation of an event in its total human reality, and they need not necessarily be taken one at a time;

(vi) *colloquy: a free, conversation-like personal prayer consisting in words and listening space, in which one speaks 'as one friend speaks with another, or a servant with a master, at times asking for some favour, at other times accusing oneself of something badly done, or sharing personal concerns and asking for advice about them' [Exx. 54]. Ignatius is insistent that Gospel contemplation should terminate with this kind of prayer (which may, of course, also arise during the contemplation itself); the prayer of colloquy at the end of contemplation has the effect of carrying the contemplation of the Gospel forwards into the here-and-now of daily life.

Repose Days

It is a standard practice in giving the full *Exercises* (20th Annotation [Exx. 20]) to allow two or three days when the exercitant comes off the full programme and has the oppor-

tunity to relax and recoup strength for the next stage. These
are generally called 'Repose Days'. Their equivalent in the
text is found in the two days in which the full programme
of *prayer is suspended, viz. the day of the Kingdom exercise [Exx. 99], and the final day of the Third Week [Exx.
208 7th day]. They also meet a concern, shown in the text in
various ways, that the exercitant avoid counter-productive
fatigue.

Practical questions regarding the distribution, organization, and régime of Repose Days need mainly to be
considered in relation to times, persons and places (cf.
[Exx. 4, 18]), and it should be stressed that there is no need
for fundamentalism in following the text of the *Exercises*.
Some basic principles, however, should always be kept in
mind. First, the two days of modified régime are days
within the retreat, not days when the retreat is suspended.
Second, as well as enabling the exercitant to recoup energies by coming off formal meditation or contemplation,
they positively advance the retreat process itself by replac-
ing formal prayer with more or less continuous reflection.

Today special allowance has to be made for the requirements of a group and how best to balance the needs of the
group and those of the individual.

While the text of the *Exercises* suggests that the exercitant remains 'separated' (*apartado* [Exx. 20]), it is the
usual practice today to suspend the silence on Repose Days.
Note in this connection that the 1599 Directory allows that
for special reasons it might be good for the director or
someone else to visit the exercitant after dinner or supper
for suitable recreation.27 The practice may seem to us
impossible, or too artificial, but the point of principle
should be noted: that some exercitants can be helped by a
certain kind of conversation. Today we prefer to make the

---

27   'The director should also consider whether for special reasons it may
     not sometimes be a good idea for either himself or some other mature
     and discreet person assigned by him to spend time with the exercitant
     immediately after dinner or supper for suitable recreation', *Directories*,
     Official Directory of 1599, ch. 6, p. 301.

possibility available on the Repose Days; clearly, break days of some kind are necessary if the exercitant is to sustain the energy level and capacity for attention necessary to make the full *Exercises*.

Riches and honour

In the *Exercises* the main disordered *desires, whether in gross or subtle forms, are the covetous desires for riches, and for the honour to which riches lead. In the speech of Lucifer the strategy is clearly spelt out, 'the first step is riches, the seond honour, and the third pride; from these three steps the enemy leads people on to every other vice' [Exx. 142]. Both riches and honour can be 'used' to promote the glory of God, but in the Weeks of the *Exercises* Ignatius is mainly concerned with the 'covetous' desire for riches and for an honour which is vain and worldly. To see why these have the wide and lethal significance he attributes to them, we must look at the way honour figures in the *Exercises*. One thing clear even on a superficial reading is that in them the desire for honour is second in a sequence of desires of which the first is the covetous desire for riches. On closer reading, it becomes apparent that riches are for Ignatius mainly significant precisely because they are the stepping stones to honour.

To some, the disordered desire for honour might seem a fairly harmless eccentricity. The reason why Ignatius can invest it with fundamental importance in the dynamic of sin is to be found in its essential relationship to God and to other people, and also to God's project in the world. As a relationship to God it displaces God by self, establishing a universe blatantly or subtly centred on the praise, and reverence, and *service not of God but of me. But honour is never just a personal or private thing; it is essentially relational. There can be no honour without other people: other people for me to honour and to give honour to me. Honour, then, is used to establish relationships, either supportive (for and with) or competitive (over against) – and in the latter case, it becomes the basis of an essential hostility – that builds Babylon where Christ wishes to build Jerusalem. Since the desire for honour is central to a strategy that extends through every human place and situation, it is reasonable to link the search for honour with the only explicit detail used by Ignatius in the Incarnation contemplation to epitomize the 'actions' of a world in need of redemption: 'to watch what the persons on the face of the earth are doing, for instance wounding and killing one another' [Exx. 108]. Wordly honour is necessarily aggressive; it is defined not as a relationship with and for people, but against people.

Service

Service can be considered a defining characteristic of Ignatian spirituality, and it is integral to the criteria proposed in the *Exercises* for every choice and orientation. The term 'apostolate' is post-Ignatian, but the concept is contained in such terms as 'helping souls', 'labouring in the Lord's vineyard', the 'labour' mentioned in the Kingdom exercise [Exx. 96], and above all in the concept of *service*. For Ignatius this is a word which carries practical implications of action and labour, but which is inseparably linked with

praise, *reverence, and glory; and it is understood by
Ignatius in a profound sense, in which action and labour is
a mode of union with Christ. For to serve Christ is to work,
not only to work *for* him, but *with* him – 'with' in the sense
that the more wholeheartedly a person responds to the call
to serve, they become God's conjoined instrument.[28]
Through his servant, his 'instrument', Christ himself
continues in the world the mission inaugurated in his mortal
life.

This mission is exercised in and through the *Holy
Spirit, poured out by Christ on his disciples, and its forms
have a diversity which reflects the freedom of the Spirit at
work through the varieties of times, persons, and places –
as the briefest survey of the Ignatian *apostolate in its
history and in its contemporary focus on justice and the
evangelization of culture, readily illustrates. However,
Ignatius is insistent that there is a typical Christ-pattern,
which will somehow appear in all authentic service, namely
the Paschal mystery, characterized especially by *poverty
and *humility in the widest sense.[29]

---

[28] '... the means which unite the human instrument with God and so
dispose it that it may be wielded dexterously by His divine hand are
more effective than those which equip it in relation to men', *Constitutions* X, 2 (§813), p. 322.

[29] '... ask God our Lord ... so that the motive for desiring or keeping
this thing or that be solely the service, honour and glory of the Divine
Majesty' [Exx. 16]; cf. [Exx. 46, 155].

Part III

The Inner World

Abhorrence

Abhorrence, a necessary but slightly dangerous affective capacity, consists in a perception of judgement, a set of the will and associated imagination and emotion, which together constitute a stable attitude of aversion or repudiation. In the *Exercises* the term occurs in three places: 'I tell you that you should love your enemies and do good to those who *abhor* you' [Exx. 278]; in the Notes on Scruples – errors of judgement that conduce to scruples are 'much to be *abhorred*' [Exx. 348]; and most importantly in the First Week colloquies, where the exercitant prays for *abhorrence* in relation to sin, disorder and the 'world' [Exx. 63].

Abhorrence of personal sin and disorder will recall Ignatius' account in the *Autobiography* of a vision of *Mary with the Christ-child, which he experienced at Loyola.[1] The vision gave rise to feelings of 'loathing' (*asco*) as he confronted his past, and had decisive subsequent effects, particularly in the realm of sexuality. Though *asco* is a slightly more emotive word than *aborrecimiento,* the text clearly casts light on the sense of abhorrence in the First Week colloquies in the *Exercises*. In relation to the 'world', the central place of abhorrence is brought out in a text in the *Constitutions* in which, expanding the doctrine of the Two Standards and the Modes of Humility, Ignatius insists on the need for total, and not merely partial, abhorrence of worldly honour, fame and 'the esteem for a great name on earth'.[2]

Though employed sparingly in both the *Exercises* and the *Constitutions*, the word represents principles basic to a radical understanding of conversion. Since abhorrence is the corollary of *desire, conversion (the Spirit-given realignment of desire) is only complete if it brings about a Spirit-given re-alignment of the capacity to abhor. To the extent to which the values of a pre-converted outlook are not turned into anti-values by conversion, conversion is

---

[1] *Personal Writings*, §10 of the 'Reminiscences', p. 16.
[2] *General Examen of Candidates*, ch. 4, §44 (tr., Ganss, pp. 107–8).

lacking in singleness of vision and motivational integrity. Thus, one is truly converted to following Christ poor only to the extent to which one feels positively and consistently averse to 'a great name on earth'. The process of conversion comes about not only through the grace of new desire, but also through the grace to experience new aversion.

We co-operate in these *graces by every means of promoting affective change: entry into previously evaded realms of experience, exposure to other people's minds, and so on. Taking this as read, the *Exercises* bring out the crucial importance of two means in particular. First, the exercitant must pray for specific Spirit-given knowledge or insight (*interno conoscimiento* [Exx. 63]); for what rouses abhorrence is not knowledge of an abstract or general character but the personal insight that penetrates to the spiritual essence of sin, and which can only be imparted by the *Holy Spirit.[3]

Second, this understanding is found in the context of growing intimacy with Christ, as he is met with in the *Exercises*, tender yet also strong and confrontational. By this relationship we are drawn into the mind of Christ, and enabled to share the vision and values, which are the roots of his 'true teaching' [Exx. 164]. The point is developed in the above-mentioned text from the *Constitutions*: 'to abhor whatever the world loves and embraces' is to 'accept and desire with all possible energy whatever Christ our Lord has loved and embraced. Just as those who follow the world love and seek ... honours, fame, and esteem for a great name on earth', so, 'those truly following Christ our Lord love and intensely desire everything opposite ... because of the love and reverence which He deserves'.[4] Aversion to what is contrary to Christ is correlative to the love-grounded desire to share the mind of Christ, so that living in him one shares his own patterns of *love and abhorrence.

---

[3] In the Exercises this insight is the object of the 'perfect knowledge' petitioned in the first Method of Prayer [Exx. 240].
[4] *General Examen of Candidates*, ch. 4, §44 (tr., Ganss, pp. 107–8).

If, however, there is an 'ordered' or 'Spirit-given abhorrence', many sentiments which could be described in ordinary language as 'abhorrence' differ quite fundamentally from the dispositions prayed for in the *Exercises*. In view of this certain cautionary points need to be made. The negative concept of abhorrence must be interpreted in relation to the positive theology of *creation which is the basis of 'finding God in all things'. The object of abhorrence is not created reality in itself but only the abuse of it. The action of the Spirit in authentic abhorrence, though on occasion it may be experienced as stressful and disturbing, is always *forward,* towards *consolation and its effects of constancy, clarity of vision, spiritual and psychic energy, freedom from inner conflict and the desire for God. As with *fear, there may be situations when it is a sentiment of abhorrence that keeps us temporarily on course, but a person whose *habitual motivation* is predominantly negative, a person controlled and energized by hate, dislike, or revulsion, is little advanced in the graced insight and attitude requested in the *Exercises*.

It should be noted that the *grace of abhorrence prayed for in the *Exercises* is a matter of stable habit and outlook. As such it will ordinarily be attained not through a single experience, however compelling, but through processes of growth and healing in which, as in the development of other graced dispositions, the imaginative and emotional components may not easily fall into line.

And notice finally that where abhorrence in relation to personal sin is concerned, a certain discernment is required in order to recognize the genuine grace in practice. Conversion involves self-confrontation; and the experience of abhorrence will include the emotional impact of this self-confrontation. But it is important that the grace, requested in the triple *colloquy and described in the *Autobiography* in connection with Ignatius' vision at Loyola, should not be presumed without more ado to be present in reactions of self disgust or psychological guilt, which neither arise from, nor lead to, 'interior knowledge', a sense of the power and mercy of God, or real commitment.

Abnegation

This is one of the terms, prominent elsewhere in Ignatius'
writings, which do not appear in the *Exercises*, even if the
concept is central to them. It can be located especially in
references to the 'conquest' (*vencer*) or overcoming of *self*
[Exx. 21, 87], and in the 'golden rule' that makes all spiritual progress conditional on the shedding 'of self-love,
self-will, and self-interest' [Exx.189]. The theme appears,
with the mention of opposing 'sensuality' and 'carnal and
worldly love', in the Kingdom [Exx. 97] and Three Classes
[Exx. 157]. It is prominent in the theme of elected
*poverty, and reaches its high point in the theme of
compassion.

Some of these texts can be read simply on a psycholog-
ical/ascetical level, as indicating a project essential for
anyone aspiring to act in interior freedom and to make
choices on higher criteria than pain and pleasure. In the
language of Ignatius, only by self-conquest can the 'lower'
faculties become ordered to will and intellect, the resistances of instinctive self-interest (the flesh) be contained,
self-will, self-love and self-interest be transcended, and
decisions made in freedom from disordered *affection. But
in the context of the *Exercises*, the asceticism of self-
conquest and self-transcendence must be understood as
integrated into the higher process of the self-denial by
which we become a new person in Christ.

Modern difficulties

Most directors of the *Exercises* will be aware, however,
that such 'self' language causes resistances today, which
are not to be dealt with simply by appealing to its scriptural
basis. The reaction is no doubt due in part to the profoundly
challenging quality of the Gospel doctrine. But there is a
further obstacle coming from the overall character of the
self-language of traditional spirituality and from ways of
behaving associated with it. This character is seemingly so

pervaded by the negative, and contains seemingly so few countervailing positive elements, that the difference from our own language and behaviour seems to amount almost to incompatibility.

This (often unstated) impression, while containing elements of truth, should not be allowed to pass without critical examination. There are elements of denial integral to the following of Christ (through passion and death into resurrection) and to the discarding of the old identity to become a new person in the Spirit. These are processes of which the ultimate agent, behind our cooperation, is the *Holy Spirit. Thus the seemingly negative *self-language* of the *Exercises* is ultimately not only psychologically positive but an invitation to be involved in the transcendent process of the Spirit leading us to the fullness of selfhood in Christ.

Self-abnegation, understood in the context of Christ's prediction of suffering ('Jesus began to show his disciples that he must go to Jerusalem and suffer many things . . .' and, 'If any man would come after me, let him deny himself and take up his cross and follow me', Matthew 16:21, 24) represents the pivotal grace of the *Exercises* as a conversion process. The essential conversion of the *Exercises* consists in making the transition between two ways of relating to Christ: the relationship which might be described as that of ordinary devotion, which is compatible with a high degree of egocentricity; and the relationship in which the centre of gravity changes, and from being centred on *self* the person becomes centred on *Christ*, a sharer in his life, and hence in his relationship with his Father and total commitment to the Kingdom. It is in the context of this transition, with its relinquishment of deep personal securities, the sense indeed of an actual loss of self, that the exercitant must try to relinquish self-love, self-will and self-interest. This transition is the key to all the points of self-confrontation in the *Exercises*: penance, the offering of the Kingdom and Two Standards, the Third Mode of Humility, the Third Week petition 'to be broken with Christ broken' [Exx. 203]. In the *Exercises* it is especially the key to the *Election, as the connection of the 'golden rule' with the Election shows; for a good and true election requires the relinquishment of self-interest, not just in order to achieve objectivity, but in order to hear and respond to God's will, and which is therefore a moment of union.

If many people now feel unhappy with the self-language of the *Exercises*, finding it one-sided (even if true) and inconsistent with the 'holistic' ethos of spirituality today, this impression is probably caused to a large degree not by what the *Exercises* actually say, but rather by an absence of countervailing positive terminology corresponding to the self-language in common currency today: cf. the ordinary meanings and use of 'selfish' and 'self-centred', as terms of disapproval, or 'self-control' and 'self-discipline', in ordinary understanding of personal growth processes; 'self-respect', 'self-esteem', 'sense of self', 'self-worth', 'good self-image', 'self-acceptance', and even, indeed, a positive view of 'self-love'. Language of this sort did not exist in the sixteenth century and it has come fully into its own only with the development of modern psychology. As regards its importance for our understanding of the *Exercises*, some simple observations may be in place.

That Ignatius does not express himself in this way does not mean that the corresponding values and insights are absent from his outlook. Rather, an examination of his writings and of his relationships would suggest that he possessed them to a considerable degree. Nevertheless there have been tendencies in the past to put interpretations on self-denial that have cripplingly restricted personal growth rather than fostered it. The general development we categorize as 'holistic' is positive and enriching, but its value should be assessed in realistic recognition of the fact that the special temptation of a culture of fulfilment is to make a virtue of egocentricity.

Affection

The 'affections' cover a range of dynamisms that give
direction, temporarily or habitually, to a person's life. They
include every attraction towards, or enjoyment of, what is
in some sense perceived as 'good', and correlatively every
recoil from or hatred towards what is, in some way,
perceived as 'bad'. The affections also include 'states'
(such as the joy and sadness characteristic respectively of
*consolation and desolation); while not necessarily being
responses to specific objects, these exercise an overall
effect on perception, judgement, and decision. The
'ordered' – or appropriately directed – affections of Ignatian spirituality are those which move a person towards the
*love of God, or in ways directed towards God's praise,
reverence, and *service. An affection can be ultimately so
'ordered' whether its immediate object is God, or whether
the term refers immediately to another relationship (with a
person, an object or situation) itself fully in harmony with
one's relationship with God.

The affective faculty operates at every level of the self.
There are thus purely instinctive affections, consisting in
immediate reactions to pain or pleasure. The affections that
primarily concern spirituality are those of the will (a term
often replaceable by 'heart'). In everyday language we
acknowledge these when we describe someone as 'committed', as 'having their heart' in something, as being 'highly
motivated' (cf. 'where your treasure is, there is your heart
also'), etc.

The affections of the will are not to be simply identified
with emotions. It is a fact of experience that a person can
be moved by the deeper affections of the will in spite of
contrary affections on the emotional level; however, the
interplay and mutual reinforcement of the affections of the
will and the emotions, are regarded by Ignatius as ordinary
(though not constant) states of affairs, and indeed one of the
important ways in which we are guided by God is precisely
through the action of the Spirit in emotion.

It would be hard to overstate the importance of the affections in Ignatian spirituality. Ordered affections provide Christian life with its energy, spontaneity, and ardour. Misdirected or 'disordered' affections, on the contrary, are one of the fundamental blocks to spiritual growth. Though the development of 'ordered' affection requires discipline, and gains much, too, from the insights of psychology, it would be a mistake to interpret Ignatius' concern with 'ordered' and 'disordered' affections too much in ascetical terms. His spirituality is about the *conversion* of the affections, a process which entails profound changes brought about by the *Holy Spirit.

The concept of affection is impossible to translate satisfactorily; something of its original sense survives in the negative term 'disaffected', but in common contemporary parlance 'affection' has lost the strong sense it bears in the vocabulary of the *Spiritual Exercises*.

Confusion

The general sense of this word is conveyed by the Second Addition [Exx. 74], where the exercitant considers the position of a faithless knight facing a king, who on his side has always been faithful and generous.[5] Confusion then is the sentiment of a sinner faced with unmerited love and mercy. In the *Exercises* it is an initial response. As such it dispels complacency, breaks down defences, and opens the way to

5 There are two other occasions when the term 'confusion' is used: in the petition of the First Meditation, where one asks for 'personal shame and confusion' [Exx. 48], and in the petition for the First Contemplation of the Passion [Exx. 193].

deeper responses to the mystery of *love and mercy. Various alternatives capture something of the connotations of 'confusion', for example, 'embarrassment'. It should be noted, however, that 'confusion' carries no overtone of *fear, as Ignatius makes clear in the *Autobiography* in describing his feelings during a storm at sea: 'He couldn't be afraid of his sins, nor of being damned, but he felt great *confusion* and sadness from judging that he had not used the gifts and graces that God our Lord had imparted to him.'[6]

Consolation and desolation

On even a perfunctory reading of Ignatius' Rules for Discernment, it becomes clear that they are largely concerned with two phenomena: spiritual consolation and spiritual desolation. The *Exercises* do not claim that we are in one or other of these situations all the time.[7] Both, however, are ordinary experiences of any serious Christian life, and such is their importance that to recognize them, to know their effects, and to be able to deal with them, is essential for the discernment of spirits and for following the guidance of the *Holy Spirit. Before asking why, we need to see what these phenomena are.

To what kinds of experience does Ignatius refer in using the terms 'spiritual consolation' and 'spiritual desolation'? Essentially they are situations in which the influence of the *spirits* makes itself felt in movements of consciousness, i.e.

---

6   *Personal Writings*, §33 of the 'Reminiscences', p. 28.
7   See [Exx. 6, 177, 208, 314] with the comments in *Understanding the Spiritual Exercises*.

in the interaction between these and our thoughts, judg-
ments, fantasies, inclinations and *desires.[8] They cover a
range of experiences, of varying degrees of emotional
intensity. Both consolation and desolation may describe
more or less prolonged moods, or reactions to a particular
stimulus or thought, a word, a project, etc. They can alternate rapidly and disconcertingly. Consolation and
desolation can interpenetrate. They can be quite powerful
experiences – a person exposed to the more challenging
aspects of the word of God in the solitude of the *Exercises*
may well find them such – but they are often very discreet
signals, which we can in fact quite easily turn away from.

Consolation and desolation as understood in the *Exercises* are by definition 'spiritual', and this qualification,
though easily misinterpreted, is crucial to the understanding
of both experiences. Two implications may be noted, one
having to do with the *object* of the experience, the other
with its *quality*.

First, whether we immediately recognize the fact or not,
both consolation and desolation are felt *reactions to God*,
to his truth and to the values of the Gospel, and to God's
here-and-now word to us, in whatever way this is mediated.
Consolation is a positive reaction; desolation is also a reaction to God, but a negative reaction, the experience of a
sensibility in some way pulling away from God, from his
truth, and from his claims on the closed realms of our
egocentricity.

Consolation and desolation are also 'spiritual' in a sense
which applies to the *quality* of the feelings themselves. As
the terms imply, consolation and desolation are in some
sense positive and negative feelings – consolation being an
experience of deep (not superficial) peace and happiness,
while the marks of desolation are (again in a deep sense)
stress, bitterness, unhappiness. But the positive and nega-

8   [Unfortunately the entry on *discernment*, though projected, was never
    written; and there is some indication that an entry on *spirits* was envis-
    aged, though not mentioned in the lists.]

tive quality characteristic of consolation and desolation is not any kind of good or bad feeling. Each has the distinctive quality of consonance or dissonance associated with the Second Time of *Election.[9]

The key to consolation and desolation as experiences lies, then, in the person's fundamental relationship to God, his or her attitude of heart towards *good* in faith, hope and love. Thus what makes consolation a 'good' experience and desolation a 'bad' one is the positive or negative relationship of the sensibility to this fundamental attitude. In consolation our sensibility, influenced by the good spirit, is in consonance with the inclination of the heart, while the particular distress of desolation is not any feeling of distress, but one reflecting a state of dissonance between the fundamental inclination of one's being and a sensibility pulled by the bad spirit.

The importance of consolation and desolation

To be able to discern consolation and desolation in one's experience, to have some comprehension of the implications of these two conditions, and to be able to handle them, is essential both for our overall growth in the Spirit, and also, within that overall growth, for the ability to discern the *will of God in concrete choices. To see this, we must look at some characteristic implications of the two situations.

The immediately obvious characteristic of consolation is an experience of *élan*, of felt love, etc. But important as this is, it does not fully explain the significance Ignatius gives to consolation. To appreciate both how consolation belongs to the ordinary processes of spiritual growth, and also the close association established by Ignatian spirituality between consolation and decision-making, two other

---

[9] 'When sufficient light and knowledge is received through experience of consolations and desolations, and through experience of the discernment of different spirits' [Exx. 176]

aspects of consolation must be taken into account. First, as well as being a time of *élan*, consolation is also a situation of perception. In consolation we are open to the word of God through scripture and prophecy. In consolation our perception of reality and our reactions to it are not distorted by our personal 'bad spirits', and we are open to hear the word of God through it. It is in consolation that we are able to perceive the specific consonance between a felt inclination and one's identity in Christ. The other aspect of consolation has to do with memory. The effects of consolation in an individual's life at any given moment come not only from present consolation. They come from the memory of consolation experienced in the past, quite particular memories, but also the effect on attitudes and judgement of a lifetime's accumulated experiences of consolation.

To see the significance of desolation, again we need to look at its implications. Desolation not only reverses the felt *desire for God and his will, characteristic of consolation, bringing in the place of these sluggishness and resistance; it is also the reverse of consolation in the qualities of perception it causes. Desolation affects perception, distorting and scrambling the ways we experience reality, and therefore the judgements we make about it (hence the need before making a decision, to discern whether we are under the influence of desolation). And, as with consolation, desolation can work on us not only in the present but from the past. Our present desire for God and openness to him is affected not only by present desolation but by the accumulation of desolate perceptions in the past.

It will be noted that in the First Set of Rules for Discernment [Exx. 313–327] desolation is more heavily emphasized than consolation, and that many of the Rules are concerned with 'going against' desolation. Desolation, like consolation, is a dynamism. Each, unless the person makes a contrary option, will tend of itself to carry the person on its own way, in consolation towards enhancement, in desolation towards a diminishment, of the quality of the Christ-life in us. But since the desolate person is more likely to follow the dynamism of desolation than a consoled person to resist the dynamism of consolation, the Rules in dealing with desolation put much emphasis on the need, and the ways, to oppose desolation and to regain the initiative.

It may be well here to touch on a general point, crucial to Ignatius' spiritual doctrine, but easily missed on a perfunctory reading of the Rules. Going against desolation is not just damage-limitation. Once a person in desolation recognizes the situation, and opts against it, the meaning changes; desolation itself becomes a way forward, offering its own possibilities for growth, its own wisdom. If past desolation is recognized and reflected on, instead of being a weight on the spirit, it becomes a source of wisdom and progress. If one goes back to the point in which meditation on the word of God aroused desolation, then the desolate reaction to the word of God, far from permanently blocking that word, may ultimately serve to reveal its challenge. The possibilities in opposed desolation complement those of consolation. If consolation is a time for vision and decision, desolation, if opposed, brings purification to our commitment and strengthens it through perseverance. Consolation teaches us to serve the Lord joyfully and with *élan*; in desolation we learn to serve him selflessly.

Desire

In the opening sentence of the *Autobiography* Ignatius describes himself on the eve of his conversion as a desire-driven personality, his predominant desire being to gain

honour through feats of arms;[10] and his conversion story is
not a story of desire repressed, but of the emergence
through conflict and crisis of desires of a changed quality
and direction. Originating in converted desire, Ignatius'
spirituality will be marked by desire as a constant and
explicitly central theme.

The desires which preoccupy him are the antithetical deep-
current desires, which he attributes to the 'good' and the
'bad' *spirits*: the desires on the one hand through which we
experience the effects of the *Holy Spirit, and those which,
whatever their immediate provenance, are 'disordered' and
influence us in ways inimical to the life of the Spirit in us. For
a full account of the operation of these desires in Ignatian
spirituality, it would be necessary to refer to the *Constitutions*, the *Spiritual Diary*, and the *Letters*, as well as the *Exercises*. In the latter spiritual and anti-spiritual desires are
treated mainly in connection with the two objectives of the
Exercises themselves: *conversion* and *decision*.

Desire and conversion

To desire is to experience need or incompleteness; and the
desire integral to the conversion process is the felt need for
God and his gifts, the sense of an incompleteness that only
these can fill.[11] Particular forms of the desire for God (the
specific graces) are specified as the *Exercises* proceed
through the stages of the conversion process: the desire to
respond to God act by act with complete integrity [Exx.
46], to experience the *graces of contrition [Exx. 55], to
come through deepening knowledge, *love, and discipleship [Exx. 104] and through participation in Christ's death
and resurrection [Exx. 203, 221] to the love which is the

---

10   'Until the age of twenty-six he was a man given up to the vanities of
     the world, and his chief delight used to be in the exercise of arms, with
     a great and vain desire to gain honour', *Personal Writings*, §1 of the
     'Reminiscences', p. 13.
11   In the *Constitutions*, steadfast and intense desire is considered the basis of
     vocation: *General Examen of Candidates*, ch. 4, §94 (tr., Ganss, p. 105).

grace of the *Contemplatio ad amorem* [Exx. 233]. The
graces of conversion also include, as centrally important,
the desire to be involved in Christ's mission [Exx.
91] and to share somehow in Jesus' own situations of *poverty and
opprobrium [Exx. 98, 147, 167]: Ignatius sees these as
inseparably connected both with personal spiritual quality
and with the effective apostolic presence that represents and
builds Jerusalem in the world [Exx. 138].

Spirit-given desires are – precisely – 'given'. We can
experience them only because, latently, they are already
there, awaiting discovery. But this does not invite total
passivity on our side. It is for us to elicit, develop and
intensify our desires through various modes of collaborative
initiative. In the *Exercises* this initiative takes two main
forms, *petition and contemplation. By articulating a desire
in petition we commit ourselves to it, even against a more
appealing or safer immediate desire (cf. [Exx. 157]). In the
contemplations of the *Exercises* (together with the various
considerations and meditations) the exercitant is provided
with vision and meaning and is drawn into a living imita-
tive relationship with Christ in which he or she comes to
desire as Christ himself desires.

The positive tone of Ignatius' treatment of desire should
not, however, obscure the reality of the other desires that
proceed from the bad or destructive spirit. As the *Exercises*
go along, particular forms of these are identified: misdirected appetite for sex [Exx. 33-37] or food [Exx.
210-217]; the forms assumed for a particular individual by
'sin', 'disorder', 'worldliness' [Exx. 63], or by '*riches
and honour' [Exx. 146]; desires which compete with the
voice of reason in decision-making [Exx. 182]. But while
recognizing disordered desire in its specific forms, we must
recognize as well the desire which is their deeper root. At
this level, disordered desire has as its goal – usually covert
– the absolutizing of the self and the virtual denial of creaturehood that constitute the capital sin of *pride.
Disordered desire thus understood not only affects the
person possessed by it; it also has a cosmic dimension,

promoting the power that works in the world against the
kingdom and builds Babylon [Exx. 140]. The final logic of
disordered desire is pinpointed in the meditation on the
Incarnation where the exercitant contemplates a world in
need of redemption; under the head of 'what the persons in
the world are doing' one is offered a single stark example:
'they kill one another' [Exx. 108].

The downward pull of disordered desire will always be
with us, and in some individuals may remain unabatingly
recalcitrant without fault on their part. But the thrust of the
action of the Spirit in a life of sincere and persevering discipleship is towards the *conversion* of desire itself, the
progressive re-alignment of desire (and aversion) at every
level to that of a person's fundamental orientation.

This process requires both the cultivation of positive
desire, and effort and initiative directed against the recalci-
trance of disordered desire in itself – hence the various
specific measures commended in the *Exercises*: *indifference; 'going against' (*agendo contra*); the *examen*;
*prayer for the grace of *abhorrence [Exx. 63]; meditation
on and option against cupidity. But necessary as these
measures are, positive desire must be their context. Negative procedures alone cannot produce the new mind and
heart that is the mark of authentic conversion. Thus every
measure in the *Exercises* aimed directly at resisting, dimin-
ishing or mastering disordered desire is taken in the context
of a programme designed to strengthen positive desire for
God and God's ways: consideration of God's blessings;
vision of God's creative purpose; gratitude for God's goodness and mercy; intense desire to know and love and follow
Jesus.

Desire and decision (choice)

Desires are crucial to the *Exercises* for the further reason
that they are a way of finding the *will of God in choices
where decision must be reached partly on subjective
grounds. In such choices, desire operates in two ways: as a

pre-condition for choice, and in some situations as the criterion of choice. The desire, which is a pre-condition for choice, is a desire to make only the choice that might be for God's greater *glory. Such a disposition supposes the various conversions of outlook and attitude that mark the stages of the exercitant's preparation for the election, especially the transcending of self-love, self-will and self-interest [Exx. 189]. Ignatius also presupposes a preference on one's own side for the 'poorer' option – a preference that must spring from *love for Christ and not from dubious psychological motivations that might give rise to such a preference.

How does a person who desires God's will, whatever it *might* be, come to the perception of one particular object or course as being God's concrete will for them here and now? Ignatius' answer to this question is the three Times of *Election, each with its own criterion or type of 'evidence' for God's will. In the Third Time, the criterion is the stronger rational case. In both the First and Second Times, however, there is an intuition contained within the desire itself. In these 'times', relevant data and lines of argument will – and indeed must – be taken into account, but what finally impels choice is something over above these, a sense of rightness inseparable from the very attraction felt for a particular course. Precisely because I desire something in a particular way, I recognize that what I desire is God's will for me.

A person truly in search of God's will may be graced to experience this quality of desire in various situations: the situation in which a person senses the leading of the Spirit in the desire for an object that would otherwise lack appeal (e.g. 'actual *poverty') or the situation in which it is possible to sense the 'love from above' transformatively present within a desire of immediate attraction (e.g. the love that prompts me to give alms to a friend or relation [Exx. 338] (cf. Exx. [184]).

Choice and 'ordinary' desire

It should not be thought that Spirit-guided desire is confined
to cases where the objects of desire are things not ordinarily found attractive. Nor is it the case that the desire quality
of the Second Time of Election is not usually to be found
in our immediate desires, the desires which arise out of the
consistency of immediate reality, with its immediate meanings and goals, the kind of desire which leads a person to
take a partner for life, to embark on a line of study, express
creativity in a certain way, to adopt or support a cause, and
so on. Certainly, such desires are easily captured into the
orbit of the covetous and carnal; yet God can so act in them
that precisely in and through our immediate desire we sense
'the love which descends from above' [cf. Exx. 184].

This said, however, it is important to realize that the idea
of finding God's will in our desires is never an easy option.
Certain attitudes mark a Spirit-inspired desire, whether
mediated or not through immediate attraction and meaning.
Where choice has to do with a life-situation, the quality of
desire will match the distinction drawn in the *Exercises*
between the desire to serve God in a situation not itself
chosen for God and the desire to choose the situation itself
for the service of God [Exx. 169]. It is the mark of a
Spirit-inspired desire that it contains an openness to transcendence, a readiness to acknowledge that in following out
one's desire one will be led to new forms of involvement
in the Paschal mystery. Hence the conditions necessary to
recognize the call of God in a desire of natural attraction
are the same conditions that are necessary to recognize in
our desire a call to literal *poverty: affective freedom, the
desire to put off self-love, self-will and self-interest, openness to the paradoxical values of a literal imitation of
Christ, and the willingness to test desire for hidden ambi-
guity (e.g. by the checks proposed in the Second Way of
the Third Time of Election [Exx. 184–187], thus to subject
it if necessary to the test that risks its own loss). It should
be added that the process of discernment may be protracted

beyond the compressed time-scale of a retreat *election, and it must always be remembered that compulsive or obsessional desires are not amenable to discernment.

Thus, the principle – that God leads through our desires – contains no invitation to assume here that every spontaneous attraction, even every attraction that immediately 'feels right', contains in fact this kind of evidence of God's leading. But if it can easily be over-simplified it remains one of the more important ways in which Ignatius' positive approach to desire contributes to the spirituality of everyday life.

Levels and categories of desire

Psychologically, desire consists in complex interactions between the spontaneous attractions and aversions of sensibility with principles and attitudes (not always consciously recognized), which come about in a context of social climate and personal memory (again not always recognized), and the countless influences coming from a social and religious milieu.

The desires of Ignatian spirituality are 'true' when they are true to God: their object is the *will of God and his purposes [Exx. 23]. They are true to God's self-revelation in Christ, who is the 'truth' and whose way is the true 'way'. Desires are true by this criterion to the extent to which their object is the desiring of God himself. In the meditations on the Kingdom [Exx. 91-98], the Two Standards [Exx. 136-147], and the Three Classes [Exx. 149-156] it is clear that the norm of our own desires is God's own desire; we praise, reverence, and serve God by desiring with him, and becoming involved in the working out of his desires. But there is another important psychological sense in which desires are 'true' or authentic, i.e. they are what they seem to be and do not serve to cover other (repressed or unacceptable) desires.

The desires of Ignatian spirituality are distinguished not only by their ultimate object but by their quality – they are 'whole-hearted'[12] and 'ardent',[13] i.e they consist in developed 'core desires' to which peripheral desires are in a process of re-aligning themselves. There are desires which do not produce changes of outlook and habit, nor lead to commitment and perseverance, etc. - even if felt with a certain immediate emotion. They blow us hither and yon, cause instability, weaken the power of core desire.

Desires of the will are desires which refuse to go away and retain their driving power even when immediate feelings draw elsewhere; they operate deep within the personality, are part of a person's very identity. Such desires can be lost, but are not lost quickly. It should be noted that shallow desires can also be intensely felt, while they last. Desires felt at the first level can be even experienced as intense feeling; the mark of their peripheral character is that, when the emotion has gone, nothing is left.[14] Moreover, core desire can be evil: the converted have no monopoly of commitment and perseverance.

Desires of the flesh are not only sexual or sensual desires, but may be desires for the immediately pleasurable, though postponement of pleasure is a mark of ordinary self-discipline, not necessarily of virtue. Their final object, however, belongs to the realms of the instinctively satisfying or pleasurable. Desires connected with the immediately pleasurable, or with avoiding what is not pleasurable, are to be distinguished from those connected with values and meanings Among our desires are those in which the *Holy Spirit, as joined to our own spirit, influences us through desires which are both ours and from God. Our deepest desire acts like a kind of drill which bores through layers of more superficial desires within us - desire for

[12] *General Examen of Candidates*, ch. 4, §94 (tr., Ganss, p. 105).
[13] *General Examen of Candidates*, ch. 4, §102 (tr., Ganss, pp. 108-109).
[14] 'Still, there was this difference: that when he was thinking about that worldly stuff he would take much delight, but when he left it aside after getting tired, he would find himself dry and discontented', *Personal Writings*, §8 of the 'Reminiscences', p. 15.

health, wealth, security, status, etc. – until it reaches the wellspring of all our desires which is God: 'You created me for yourself...'. When we choose according to our deepest desires the decision resonates in our psyche; when we choose contrary to our deepest desires, there is dissonance.

If desire is to be taken seriously as God's way of leading us, it is important to realize that the sheer strength of emotion attaching to a desire is no guarantee of authenticity. Certainly the desires of the Spirit are whole-hearted; of their nature, therefore, they overflow into the passions and will ordinarily have been experienced at some time as uncomplicated feelings that take us over and transform awareness. Indeed, Ignatius expects that a retreatant will ordinarily experience his or her desires in this way. (Note that 'ordered' desire does not mean 'tidy' or 'moderate' desire!) But consisting essentially in an energy and hunger in the will, authentic desire is not to be evaluated just in terms of the ebb and flow of passion. Our most authentic desires are not always the most strongly felt, certainly not in the case of *desolation.

Desire and change

Desire produces the vision that makes a future possibility already real, since it gives the energy by which to realize the possibility, the break with past attachments that impeded movement forward.

This desire for God is also for Ignatius the desiring of a person who in and with Christ works out his relationship with God in and through three conditions which constitute human reality:

1. as a person capable of infidelity and abuse of freedom, and with a concrete history of these;
2. as a person who exists in a situation of continuous interaction with the material world and with human society;
3. as a person called to serve God not only in the pursuit of

personal perfection but in bringing about the establishment
of Christ's kingdom in the world.

Given this situation, the essential implications of an authentic desire for God are presented in the ordered sequence of
petitioned *graces in the Exercises.
The change in Ignatius that took place at Loyola was not
so much in his doing anything, but in his desires; new
desires had replaced the old, and for the moment, pending
the translation of his desires into action, it could be said
that it was his new desires more than anything else that
constituted the new Ignatius: desires to imitate the saints
and to serve God. These were desires of such power that
the old desires, which made the former Ignatius, began to
fade away. In trying to change him, his brother tried
precisely to change his desires.[15] Later he had to discern
between various desires, as in the incident with the Moor[16]
Clearly he was a man led by desire, though desire had to
be discerned.

We elicit a desire when we experience a desire in germ,
or if we are not quite sure even of that, we at least 'desire
a desire' [cf. Exx. 157]. In these situations desire is a spark
and a spark requires to be fanned, as Paul tells Timothy to
fan into life the spark of the ordination received in the
laying on of hands (2 Tim. 1:6). A large part of the spirituality of desire consists in eliciting desires in this sense,
but it is essential that muscular or Pelagian people don't be
seduced into forcing emotions. Here too the main work is
that of the Spirit, and our eliciting is a union in the eliciting of the Spirit. The other response to a desire is simply
to stay with it: to stay with the desire of God or with any
other Spirit-given desire, even if we are not sure where it
may lead us, or not sure whether this is the moment to ask

---

[15] 'His brother took him to one room and then another, and with many
warnings began to beg him not to throw himself away ... all with the
purpose of detaching him from the good desire he had', *Personal Writings*, §12 of the 'Reminiscences', p. 17.
[16] *Personal Writings*, §15 of the 'Reminiscences', p. 19.

that question. With regard to the desire for God, staying with that desire, so long as the desire is sincere, is the key to *prayer at all times.

Development of desire in the Exercises

The fundamental desire, the desire for God, which is the root of all others and the criterion of their authenticity, is expressed in various ways but consists fundamentally in the desire that one's entire being, all one's affective dynamisms, and every act whether interior or external be directed to the end for which one is made, 'to praise, reverence and serve God our Lord, and by so doing to save his or her soul' [Exx. 23]. Such a desire implies the need, and creates the capacity, for a certain freedom in relation to immediate desire until it becomes clear what in fact, in one's own case or in a particular situation, conduces more to the 'end' which is the object of ultimate desire. The desire for God is the norm of all other desires. It is the most fundamental of the desires of the Spirit. For St Augustine it is the key to prayer at all times: 'We cannot constantly pray on our knees, prostrate our bodies, or raise our hands, but there is a prayer which goes on constantly, and that is desire. If you wish not to interrupt your prayer, never cease to desire.'

This fundamental desire is also the norm of all other desires, and it works out through specific desires, called by Ignatius 'ordered' desires. Ordered desires are crucial to the dynamic of the *Exercises*, both as a process of personal growth in Christ and as a way of finding God's will in concrete choices; for implicit in both processes is the principle that God's gifts are preceded by desire. That is to say, it is characteristic of God that before giving us a grace or calling us to a situation, God gives us a desire for these, not a superficial desire, nor necessarily a desire without complicating inner conflict, and certainly not superficially emotional desire, but a deeply felt hunger and sense of incompleteness that only the eventual 'finding' of the

desired object can assuage. Thus the gifts and callings of
God, precisely because desired, are experienced as connatural to us, not as extrinsic impositions; moreover,
paradoxical situations of discipleship which would be
oppressive by themselves become through desire life-giving
ways of imitating Christ. It need hardly be added that
Spirit-given desires are truly our own desires, indeed the
most genuinely personal of all the desires we experience.

Both within and outside the *Exercises* desires that
promote the dynamics of personal growth arise spontaneously, i.e. one gets in touch with the desires which
indicate God's leading and invitation without any directives
as to what these desires should be. The *Exercises*, however,
are characterized by a series of desires which may at first
sight appear to be imposed desires but which, like the
desires expressed in the prayers of the liturgy, consist in
Spirit-given desires inherent in Christian faith, hence as
already present, however obscurely, in anyone who is
living by faith. These desires are for *graces of conversion,
which include the grace of *aborrecimiento* (*abhorrence).
This is an important concept because it shows that in the
Exercises the direction of grace is to change ill-ordered
affections, not just to give strength to resist them. This
conversion of the affections does not imply that unconverted affections of one kind or another do not continue to
afflict even the converted; the experience of unconverted
desire is one of the classic forms of desolation. But the
thrust of the *Exercises* as a spirituality of desire is to the
changing of destructive desires into a deeply felt repugnance in relation to things that seemed previously
attractive, and it should be noted that this repugnance is
itself an experience of *consolation.

The desires of the First and Second Weeks culminate in
the desire for *poverty, unconditional in respect of actual
poverty, conditional in respect of material poverty and the
poverty of humiliation. Aroused by the contemplation of
Christ's mortal life and expressed especially in the Triple
Colloquies, their object is to be admitted in some way to a

more literally Christ-like situation. The poverty in which
this situation consists is desirable precisely as poverty: one
does not desire a close relationship with Christ in spite of
the poverty this might entail. However, it is desirable
because of the relationship with Christ, of which it is an
integral dimension and which transforms its meaning. One
key to the desire for poverty in the Exercises is provided
by Ignatius' own life, the vision of La Storta, in which he
is admitted in some new way to the *service of the cross-
bearing Christ. He experiences this as answering to a
prayer he has been making for some time to Our Lady, 'to
be placed with Christ'.[17]

Final comments

On the subject of desire, there is a distinction of emphasis
among classic spiritual writings corresponding to the negative (apophatic) and the positive (cataphatic) schools.[18] The
former put the stress on desire as obstacle, something to be
transcended, while the latter present desire as an essential
component in the dynamism of the Spirit. The two should
not be too widely separated, since each recognizes the
distinction formulated by Ignatius in terms of ordered and
ill ordered desire. Thus *apatheia* is concerned essentially
with desires which are an obstacle to moral and spiritual
progress and to the attainment of inner peace; authentic
apatheia in fact is ultimately not about the suppression of
desire but about its orientation, a point easily overlooked on
a casual or selective reading of an author such as St John
of the Cross. As much as any other master, Ignatius is
aware of the need to be free from the influence of the ill-
ordered desire, to control it, and eventually indeed to
convert it to its opposite. The spirituality of Ignatius is a
classic example of explicit and systematic concern with the
multiple function of ordered desires in the life of the spirit.

[17] *Personal Writings*, §96 of the 'Reminiscences', p. 60 with note 153.
[18] See *mysticism.

Devotion

Though found only four times in the Spanish text of the Exercises[19] *devoción* is one of the key words of the Ignatian vocabulary.[20] In the epilogue of the *Autobiography* he himself indicates both its personal importance and just meaning by observing that, 'after he had begun to serve God', he had grown continually 'in devotion', adding that he meant by the term 'facility in finding God'.[21]

One could add that the term particularly specifies the experience of finding God as one in which 'magnanimity and liberality' [Exx. 5] overflow into feelings. In both Latin versions, the *Vulgata* and the *Versio Prima*, 'find devotion' translates the phrase 'find what I want' of the Spanish Autograph; thus in prayer one should 'rest until satisfied' at the point where one has found devotion ('the devotion sought' according to the *Vulgata*). Devotion is an aspect of *consolation, an experience we have no power on our side to arouse or sustain and which we must not put down to our own account.

---

[19]   Thus, 'spiritual desolation gives us true knowledge and understanding, so that we may perceive within ourselves that on our part we cannot arouse or sustain overflowing *devotion* . . . but that all this is a gift and grace from God our Lord. So we are not to build our nest where we do not belong . . . and putting down to our own account *devotion* or other forms of spiritual consolation' [Exx. 322]; and cf. [Exx. 199, 252].

[20]   [The author acknowledges his debt to Alfonso de la Mora, 'La devoción en el espíritu de san Ignacio', CIS, Rome 1982.]

[21]   *Personal Writings*, §99 of the 'Reminiscences', p. 63.

Fear

Fear is a major strand in human experience and one of the functions of spiritual direction, both outside and within the practice of the Exercises, is to help people deal with it. Fear may be defined as a reaction of recoil or *abhorrence in relation to something perceived as dangerous or unpleasant. Feelings of fear without a specific object are generally described as 'anxiety'. Fears differ in kind and intensity, depending on the kind of damage or unpleasantness entailed by the feared situation, and also of course according to whether the situation is likely or imminent, remote or easy to avoid. There are fears grounded in reality and fears conjured up by *imagination; and again there are fears which belong to the human condition (e.g. the fear of death and of pain) and others are linked with values and attitudes, such as certain fears mentioned in the *Exercises* – the fear of hardship or loss of worldly honour [Exx. 9]. Fear is a natural reaction, not something in itself to be deplored; but because of its potential power, no one, who has not developed the ability to control fear or override its demands, can be free to live by higher values. And still, there are times when fear puts us in touch with realities we might otherwise overlook, and then we do well to freely choose to follow the evasive promptings arising from fear.

Servile or filial fear

In the Rules for Thinking with the Church, Ignatius distinguishes between two kinds of fear which have God himself as object, i.e. servile and filial fear [Exx. 370]. Since many people feel uncomfortable with the idea of fear as being a *positive* constituent of a relationship, it is necessary to clarify the meaning of these terms and to ask how they might speak to people today.

Servile fear

The basis of servile fear is the truth that sin is intrinsically open to its consequences and that forgiveness is gratuitous, not a necessary sequel of sin. Sin does not *demand* grace, nor should one think that sin is 'a trick of God's love that He uses to show us our poverty and creaturehood, so that He can then show us how merciful He is'.[22] Recognition of the consequences of sin is, therefore, an element in the Christian attitude towards sin. In a person in whom the higher motive of *love is weak, this recognition can give rise to a self-interested fear that inhibits the expression of even powerful sinful desires, or, in relation to sin already committed, prompts the sinner to turn to the mercy of God in repentance, albeit self-interested. In the case of such a person, servile fear goes directly against one of the major impediments to a persevering morality or to basic serious-ness and purpose in repentance, namely, the attitude of presumption on God's mercy; such a presumption obscures the real sense both of sin and of God's goodness, as distinct from a trust in mercy based on the true sense of both.

In Ignatius' time, conversion through servile fear was repu-diated by Luther as hypocritical; Catholic tradition, affirmed by Ignatius, recognized the value of such fear, but also its limitations. Its value is explained in the *Exercises*: to provide a kind of emergency brake, if the quality of love declines [Exx. 65]; to prepare for the desires of love by preventing the desires against love from being acted out [Exx. 370].

Since, however, fear does not change *desire, but only inhibits the expression of it, fear does not bring complete peace, still less radical conversion of heart: the person who 'does good deeds from fear ... has not entirely departed from evil, because she is sinning even in this; that she would sin, if she could do so without punishment'.[23] Love

---

22   Karl Rahner, *Spiritual Exercises*, p. 36.
23   St Gregory the Great, *Commentary on Job*, I, 2.36 [Office of Readings, 8th Sunday], Library of the Fathers, *Morals on the Book of Job*, I, xxvi, §37. vol. 1, Oxford, 1844, p. 52.

on the other hand, can change a person's very desires and hence bring about deep conversion.

A fear-based spirituality is, therefore, not only shallow, but necessarily stressful, involving as it does the constant frustration of a desire that one dares not meet, but which never loses its force. However, an additional note to be borne in mind is that 'servile' is probably an unhelpful adjective; the fear referred to is certainly 'fear' in the ordinary sense of the word, but it is a fear experienced within *faith*, albeit in a situation of minimal love; the implication of cravenness carried today by the word 'servile' hardly suits the climate of faith. The point is that 'fear' in the everyday sense of the term can have its place as an aid to fidelity, and that this should not be scorned.

Filial fear

In contrast to servile fear, filial fear is a quite different concept. The key to it is found in the nature of filial **love* of God – a love in which the one loved is greater, indeed, infinitely greater, than the lover, yet a love which is characterized by *affection, intimacy, and even union. Moreover, it is marked in a high degree by the quality which in some way belongs to all love, the attitude of *reverence. For a person who loves in this way, to offend or betray the other or to violate reverence are repugnant in themselves, and hence the possibility of incurring them is something to be feared. Filial love, therefore, is grounded in love and reverence, and it finds expression in worship and praise, and in an attitude towards sin based not on one's own interests, but on a vision of sin in relation to the goodness and greatness of God.

The distinction is clear in principle. But in order to apply it to life in general and to the *Exercises* in particular, one must realize that the distinction between the two kinds of fear in the Rules 'towards a true attitude of mind within the Church' [Exx. 370] is conceptual and schematic, and that it is included there not in order to provide a *key* to the *Exer-*

cises, but to affirm a contested point of doctrine.[24] In practice, no simple distinction can be drawn between a situation of 'pure' servile fear (i.e. a situation in which love is totally ineffective and fear alone is an effective motive) and the 'purely' filial fear of 'pure' love. As the scholastics saw, between these two poles there is an intermediate situation in which both fears are present, a measure of servile fear co-existing with the beginnings of a love, which if it develops fully will dissolve such fear.

It is through this that the exercitant proceeds from the opening meditation of the First Week to the highpoint of love in the *Contemplatio ad amorem*. Within the *Exercises* themselves a purely servile fear (by definition a situation in which love is not an effective force) is not one of the anticipated *graces. From the First Week on, the *Exercises* unfold totally in trust in God's loving mercy, and thus even in the Fifth Meditation (on hell) the exercitant does not experience servile fear in anything like a pure form. In this meditation one asks to experience an interior sense of the situation of damnation (which is the basis of servile fear, but not identical with it) in order that one might be protected by actual servile fear in the event of ever losing sight of God's love. The other passage, which might appear to induce purely servile fear (the 'second addition' [Exx. 74]), has in fact the effect of highlighting God's mercy.[25]

Reverential fear

When we speak of the 'loving and reverential' fear of God, considered a special gift of the *Holy Spirit, the word 'fear' has a different sense from the sense of the word in the

24 Cf. Terence O'Reilly, 'El tránsito del temor servil al temor filial en los "Ejercicios Espirituales"' (ed.) Juan Plazaola *Las Fuentes de los Ejercicios Espirituales de San Ignacio*, Bilbao, 1998, pp. 223–40.
25 '... note that from experiencing oneself as a sinner confronting justice and death, the exercitant moves into a meditation which concludes with the gratitude of a sinner forgiven and granted life (cf. [Exx. 61])', *Understanding*, pp. 66–7.

expression 'servile fear', even when one has removed from such fear misleading associations of the word 'servile'. But even with regard to 'filial' fear or the 'fear of the Lord' which is grace, it should be realized that people today are not always helped by certain analogies. Though the concept of 'filial' fear must be based, like every other aspect of our relationship with God, on analogies, it is important to realize that the reality transcends our analogies, and should not be tied too closely to styles of relationship of other cultures than ours. And yet, all authentic relationships provide analogies for the respect and *reverence which are integral to our relationship with God.

Humility

It is important not to be put off by the associations the word 'humility' carries today of something self-denigratory or servile. In the Two Standards and the Three Kinds of Humility the word sums up the whole quality of the individual's relationship to God. Humility is in fact *love, love specified as self-forgetful and focused on the other, the love that wants simply that God be God. Some very early retreat notes (attributed to Dr Ortiz and his brother) dating from the period when Ignatius had been elected General (1541) actually refer to the Degrees of Humility as 'three kinds and degrees of love of God and of desiring to obey, imitate and serve his Divine Majesty'.[26] The essential spirit of humility is captured in the remark that ends the advice on

26 MHSI, *Exercitia spiritualia S. Ignatii de Loyola*, Nova editio, vol. 100, Rome, 1969, p. 635.

'the amendment and reform of one's personal life and state': 'a person will make progress in things of the spirit to the degree to which they divest themselves of self-love, self-will, and self-interest' [Exx. 189].

In interpreting the Three Modes of Humility, and especially the third, one might suppose that Ignatius is encouraging the exercitant in the adoption of an *agendo contra* attitude of mind, but . . .

> What Ignatius is asking of us is not to imagine a real situation, but rather to abstract from a real situation and to ask what can happen when Christ and holy people confront real evil . . . He is reminding us . . . that the light of grace can shine more clearly in an evil situation. He is inviting us to desire the situation that makes that reality possible, without condoning the evil. This disposition might open up some possibilities in the *election that follows, possibilities that we might otherwise recoil from. A contemporary way of asking the question might be to think of situations where human holiness has been confronted with real evil, leave aside our judgements and our horror at the elements of evil, sin, and stupidity that are around, and instead focus on the fact that there are resources in the human condition under God that enable us to bring great fruit out of negative and painful situations in ways that could not arise in any other context.[27]

---

[27] Quotation from unpublished notes by Philip Endean presented at a workshop at St Beuno's, 2000 (he added the example of the German Jesuit Alfred Delp who died in a Nazi concentration camp); cf. Philip Endean, *Karl Rahner and Ignatian Spirituality*, Oxford 2001, pp. 122–3.

Imagination

Imagination is the capacity to be *present*, through creativity, empathy, vision or dream, to what is absent: *present* to situations which existed once, exist elsewhere, never existed or might come to exist. Its function is complementary, not opposed, to that of reason, but it is no 'back-up' faculty. On the contrary, imagination is an indispensable means of dealing with the real, to which it gives its own unique access. Approaches to imagination differ widely, however, according to culture or personal standpoint. Where rationality, control and stability are dominant values, its significance tends to be muted by insistence on caution and by allusions to 'fancy', or 'mere' imagination. On the other hand, schools of thought influenced by such factors as the Romantic movement, the demise of the classical world view, or developments in psycho-analysis, display a high appreciation of the role of imagination in a complete human life. On both sides, uncritical and oversimple extremes are to be found.

Ignatius' own position belongs to a tradition which combined open-eyed awareness of the ambivalence of imagination with a profound respect for its place in the action of the *Holy Spirit. He is keenly aware of the potential for harm in a 'disordered' imagination; but his spirituality is characterized by a positive view of imagination as a channel through which God works in human life, both in the personal processes of growth and conversion and also in the processes by which, through individuals, God builds his kingdom in the world. In the view of one leading authority, a distinctive characteristic of Ignatius' mysticism of *service is the degree to which it extends the effects of infused contemplation precisely into the faculties of action, 'such as memory and imagination'.[28]

---

[28]   de Guibert, p. 56.

Imagination in the Exercises

In the *Exercises* the imagination functions in two main
ways: in the form of the deliberate 'exercise' and as an
unsolicited phenomenon, something that 'happens'. In the
first case, the freedom and spontaneity proper to imagination as a faculty operate within pre-determined limits and
on set material (e.g. one imagines the shape and furnishings
of a room); the second corresponds to the thoughts Ignatius
describes as coming 'from outside' ourselves [Exx. 32] (we
would prefer to say, from 'somewhere inside' ourselves)
and to which the recipient of such experience must respond
with reflection, discernment and choice. In each of these
modes, imagination holds a central position in the realms
not only of *prayer but also of discernment and *election.

Imagination and prayer

There are many ways in which imagination is a constituent
element in the various exercises. The 'composition' is
either an imagined place or an imagined spiritual situation
[Exx. 47]. The concluding exercise of the First Week is in
an imaginative exercise on damnation [Exx. 66–70]. The
introduction to the Kingdom exercise requires an imaginative response to Ignatius's chivalrous parable [Exx. 92].
Other sectors, without referring to specific texts or incidents, contain material similar to that of the Gospel
contemplations: the Christ of the second and substantial
part of the Kingdom [Exx. 95], the graphically contrasted
figures of Christ and Lucifer in the 'meditation' of the Two
Standards [Exx. 140]. At their very outset, in the *colloquy
of the *Cross [Exx. 53], the *Exercises* introduce an imaginative contemplation of exactly the same kind as will be
made in the subsequent Weeks. Another kind of imaginative exercise is the Second Method of Election in the Third
Time [Exx. 184–187].

But it is with the contemplations of the Gospel in the
Second to Fourth Weeks that imagination is especially asso-

ciated. This way of prayer consists, essentially, in the experience of a Gospel narrative such that in and through the experience one encounters in contemplation the living Christ of the now. Through imagination the narrated event becomes in a sense a personal event, somewhat like an event of one's own past re-lived in memory. And it is precisely in and through the encounter with the Christ of this Gospel event, as experienced in imagination, that the living and risen Christ communicates to the exercitant here-and-now, drawing them into a deepening knowledge and love of himself and a deepening commitment to discipleship.

Imaginative contemplation, then, is a *prayer in which a creative faculty is placed at the service of the word of God, a revelatory 'given' which it must explore, expand and make personal. For such prayer to happen, it is essential both that the text remains its basis, and that imagination enjoy freedom and spontaneity, and the capacity to engage the whole person, to which it belongs as a faculty. Imagination must therefore be text-grounded without being text-bound, and two implications call especially for mention. First, it is the role of the imagination to make present to the senses the physical realities of Incarnation as manifest in a particular narrated event, the words and actions of Jesus and the places and people which contextualize them. But secondly, it is of the nature of imaginative contemplation to produce unsolicited images and experiences that do not immediately correspond to the details of the text, but have to do, rather, with positive or negative elements of personal reaction and response – e.g an implicit image of Christ born of prayer memories and past spiritual experience, or resistances and fears, perhaps previously unacknowledged, that can provide the 'desolation points', which the very process of contemplation must confront and process, cf [Exx. 62, 118].

Imagination is also, however, ambivalent. The very faculty that can give access to contemplation can serve in various ways to evade contemplation. Imagination can evade the central point of a Gospel story, by battening onto fringe details, or by fantasies that overlay rather than lead into the Gospel text. One implication of such a situation concerns the exercitant's 'personal image of Christ'. One of the ordinarily enriching effects of imagination is to bring this into play; but imagination divorced from control, input or influence from objective mediations of God's word, can give this personal image the status of an absolute, evading its need for continuous growth. Evasive possibilities are also latent in the capacity of the imagination to open up hidden layers of the mind and hence to advance self-knowledge. Today the influence of psychology has caused a heightened and generally valuable awareness of the need to integrate the non-rational elements of the self into the life of the spirit, while at the same time clarifying the ways in which imagination can advance this process. In the case of imaginative contemplation, however, the very importance of this awareness can lead to a pre-occupation with one aspect of this prayer which can limit its full range and development, and even deflect its basic purpose. Imagination can also impede the movement by which contemplation moves increasingly into focus and receptivity: having found what is sought, the exercitant is encouraged to remain 'without any anxiety to move on ... until satisfied' [Exx. 76], but a restless or hyper-active imagination tends to override this principle, and then an imaginative activity which may at first have been an aid to contemplation ends by impeding its progress.

Both the exercitant and the director must be alive to these possibilities. But the need for a few caveats in no way depreciates a prayer in which imagination takes us beyond the constrictions of immediate reality into the world of Christ's mortal life, there to meet the living Christ at a point where his history and ours intersect.

Imagination, discernment and election

In the text of the *Exercises* the word 'imagination' is used almost exclusively in relation to *prayer; in the Rules for

Discernment it occurs once only [Exx. 314], and not at all
in the section on *Election. Imagination is a central issue,
however, in both of these themes, and to fail to appreciate
this is to miss a major key for understanding the doctrine
of the *Exercises* and applying it to ordinary life-situations.

In discerning the spiritual quality of our various 'movements of consciousness', it is crucial to recognize that a
significant but often disregarded factor in these movements
is the desolate or the consoled imagination. Thus, there will
in general be a large influence of the imagination in the
'thoughts that spring from desolation' [Exx. 317] with their
characteristic false images of God, and distorted perceptions of reality. In so far as these thoughts bear on the past
they will be marked by the ways a desolate imagination
turns memory into a source of anxiety or discouragement.
Desolate thoughts about the future focus on the other hand
on imagined pleasures of a life moving away from Christ
and the imagined ordeal-like quality of a life moving
towards him [Exx. 314-315].[29] But imagination is integral
to the movements of the good spirit as well: the thoughts –
about God, self, others and the world – that arise from
*consolation [Exx. 317], the consoled memories that
strengthen faith, hope and *love (e.g.[Exx. 234, 318]) or
the consoled anticipation of the future which looks ahead
not with unreal optimism (cf [Exx. 14]), but without
groundless fears and with courage, strength and inspiration
given by the Spirit [Exx. 315].

When we turn to the decision-making processes
summarised in the *Exercises* under the three Times of Election, we find imagination appearing in the form of both
'exercise' and 'vision'.

As noted above, one of the 'methods' is an imaginative
exercise in itself, namely, the Second Method of the Third
Time, in which an emerging inclination is checked for
possible hidden motives by a series of 'what if?' questions:

---

[29] See also *Reminiscences*, §20, and *Letter to Teresa Rejadell*, §5,
Personal Writings pp. 21-2, 130.

what if I were advising another ... or were at the point of
death ... or facing judgement? [Exx. 185–187]. For an
exercitant making an election in the Second Time, Ignatius
would suggest that a helpful imaginative exercise might
consist in bringing the various possible choices before God
like a court servant laying alternate dishes before a prince,
'and noting which of them is to his liking'.[30]

In those exercises, imagination is used as an *aid* to
discernment. But imagination has also the more fundamental role in the election process of providing the very
material of discernment. To find such situations illustrated
in Ignatius' own experience, it is sufficient to refer to his
conversion and to the decisions made in its wake, as
described in the *Autobiography*.[31] In every case, the
process of decision begins with an idea or imagined project
'coming to mind' or 'offering itself': a socially impossible
courtship [§6], imitation of the saints and pilgrimage
[§§7–9], joining the Carthusians [§11], avenging the
honour of Our Lady with dagger-strokes [§15], a vigil of
arms on lines suggested by Amadís de Gaul [§17], and at
the end of the crisis of scrupulosity, the 'vision' of a dish
of meat accompanied by an urge to abandon his practice of
abstinence [§27]. In each case the situation or project is not
an abstract idea, but an emotionally charged experience,
albeit an experience of imagination; and it is the imaginatively experienced situation or project which is subjected to
the testing which leads sometimes to acceptance, sometimes
to rejection.[32]

In the *Exercises*, the principles implicit in these experiences are encapsulated in the Second and First Times of
Election. In the Second Time the object of discernment is
precisely a vision, an imagined possible situation, and the
discernment process consists in sensing through reactions of

---

[30] *Directories*, p. 9.
[31] *Personal Writings*, §§6–13, pp. 14–17.
[32] In one case, however, there is no period of testing: knowledge that it
     was God's will that he should eat meat was simultaneous with the vision
     itself [§27, p. 25].

*consolation or desolation whether or not the particular vision is of the *Holy Spirit. In the First Time, too, (generally presumed to be exemplified in Ignatius' vision of meat) it is an imagined possibility that provides the 'shown object' of choice, but a possibility known now with instant clarity to represent God's *will (cf. [Exx. 175]).

Imagination and reason in reciprocal relationship.

In connection with the place of imagination in the *Exercises*, it should be noted that for Ignatius the functions of imagination and reason are reciprocal. Examples of this are easy to find in the *Exercises*. When an exercitant in high consolation is bent on a decision that bears the marks of euphoria rather than of the Spirit, the person's imagined self-estimate must be set against considerations of practicality and reason [Exx. 14]. The imagination-based distortions that obscure moral judgement are to be countered by the rational process of *synderesis* [Exx. 315]. The effects of desolation (and hence of its potent imaginative component) must be resisted by the use of all one's 'powers' [Exx. 321], which include the power of reason. As already noted, an imaginative exercise can serve to complement the reason-based approach to election, and an exercitant contemplating the Gospel must balance the spontaneity of imagination against the 'given' character of the text. These checks and balances make us aware that neither imagination nor reason are autonomous and unaccountable, but where imagination is concerned Ignatius' recognition that imagination is indeed an ambivalent power does not diminish the positive view of its complex and irreplaceable position in the action of the Spirit.[33]

---

[33] [Quite unusually a bibliography of the sources used for this entry was added: Ferlita, Ernest C., 'The Road to Bethlehem', *Studies in Jesuit Spirituality*, 29/5, November 1997; Kolvenbach, Peter Hans, 'Images and Imagination in the Ignatian Exercises', *CIS* [=Centrum Ignatianum Spiritualitatis], vol. xviii [54], 1987, pp. 11–32; McLeod, Frederick

Indifference

A key-word in Ignatius' vocabulary, but a word which is easily misunderstood; indeed the ordinary associations of the word 'indifference' are not completely helpful for understanding this crucial, though discreetly deployed, word in the vocabulary of Ignatian spirituality.[34] Various points therefore should be noted:

1. In the *Exercises* the word is ordinarily used of a disposition of a person facing a choice.[35]
2. While 'indifference' *implicates* the emotions, it *consists* essentially in a state of will and judgement, not a state of emotion. There could come a situation where emotion was such as to make indifference for the moment impossible, and the ideal emotional climate in which to be indifferent is that which defines the Third Time of Election:[36] faced with alternative possibilities of choice, it is possible to withhold commitment of will and avoid decisive judgement with regard to either, without necessarily being free from felt attraction towards one side or repugnance for the other.
3. Indifference is not only *negative*. Suspension of immediate *desire is made possible by a higher desire. Thus indifference should not be thought of as a mental 'state' in its own right, but also as part of the experience of a relationship. As a relationship it is a 'listening-place' before the word of God.

G., 'The Use of the Imagination in the Ignatian Exercises', *CIS*, vol. xviii [54], 1987, pp. 33–92; Sheldrake, Philip, *Images of Holiness: Explorations in Contemporary Spirituality*, London [Darton, Longman and Todd], 1987 (see ch. 8, 'Imagination and Prayer'); Spear, Linda, 'When you Pray: *With Images*', *The Way*, July 1973, pp. 236–44; Walsh, James, 'Application of the Senses', *The Way Supplement*, 27, Spring 1976, pp. 59–68.]

34 The adjective 'indifferent' occurs only rarely in the *Exercises* [Exx. 23, 157, 170].

35 However, the word is also used once [Exx. 170] to indicate the moral quality of objects of choice.

36 '... one of tranquillity ... I call this a "tranquil" time in the sense that it is a situation when the soul is not moved by various spirits and has the free and tranquil use of her natural powers' [Exx. 177].

4. One has to distinguish indifference as *capacity* and as *act*: the *act* of indifference belongs to times of uncertainty as to God's word to oneself, a doubt which makes possible the discovery that leads to commitment. The *capacity* remains within the commitment.
5. Before the objects of choice, and in relation to them, indifference is not something *passive*; it is the stance that makes it possible to experience appropriate positive doubt and even a productive anxiety.
6. When the *will of God is found in the waiting space of indifference, our attitude towards whatever we perceive to be God's will becomes the *dedication* of will and of all the forces of the personality that constitute commitment. Thus, if a conscious sustained option is required to maintain the motivational integrity of commitment it is essentially that of right *intention. To the extent that a commitment is intrinsically mutable, indifference towards it remains as a *capacity*, a readiness to hear a new word should God initiate change. But the capacity to question a commitment with indifference, should the need arise, does not weaken commitment. In living out our commitments *active* indifference operates in relation to the countless ways in which we are confronted by immediate challenges to our freedom.
7. It should be noted, finally, that indifference is not exactly the same as the *détachment* which was to become central to the French spirituality of the seventeenth century.

Inner/Interior

The *Exercises* refer to an *inner* 'feeling and relish of things'
[Exx. 2], to *inner* 'knowledge of my sins' [Exx. 63] and 'of
the Lord who became human for me' [Exx. 104], to an
interior 'sense of the suffering undergone by the damned'
[Exx. 65], to the need to ask for *interior* 'suffering . . . on
account of the great suffering that Christ endured for me'
[Exx. 203] and to *interior* 'happiness' [Exx. 316].

The modern reader should realize that in these texts the
words 'inner/interior' are not a redundancy of style, but an
indication that knowledge, understanding and feeling admit
of significantly different levels. Thus on one level, *knowledge* is knowledge of facts or 'knowing about' (cf. the
'much knowledge' [Exx. 2]); *understanding* means perception of a purely intellectual kind; *feeling* an essentially
transient, even if powerful, sentiment leaving no permanent
effects. The level designated by *interior* is below and
deeper than this. Interior knowledge of one's sins contains
insight into the very nature of sin; again, to come through
the Gospels to know Jesus interiorly is to know as a friend
or lover knows, with the knowledge inseparable from being
in relationship. At the *interior* level, *knowledge* in the sense
of 'understanding' is not just intellectual perception, but the
personal vision that belongs to wisdom, and *feeling* is a way
of intuition, insight or empathy. At this deeper level, today
sometimes referred to as the 'heart', *love grows, commitments are formed, conversion comes about.

Ignatius notes that one asks for *interior* 'knowledge of all
the good I have received, so that . . . I may be able to love
and serve his Divine Majesty in everything' [Exx. 233].
That does not just sum up the grace of a particular exercise:
the Contemplation to attain Love is a kind of rehearsal for
life. It points to a possibility, made available to us by God's
grace, to live all the time this way, sensing God present in
everything, so that giving thanks for everything becomes
matter for love and *service.

Intention

The approach of Ignatius to the subject of 'intention' is characterized by two related concerns, both connected with the apostolic way of life that colours Ignatian spirituality in its entirety: decision making, and the daily situations of an active and exposed life. The place of decision in his spirituality leads Ignatius especially to emphasize the distinction between God-directed intention, as a general aspiration, and the effective motivation of a particular choice. It is important to establish the place of intention in the situations of daily life because these correspond to the category of '*all things', where the apostle either 'finds God' or is trapped in a divided life. The extent to which the apostle can in truth be the 'instrument' wielded by God, because united with God, depends first and foremost on a quality of integrity and genuineness, which in the end is what right intention is about.

According to the *Exercises* the retreatant begins every *prayer with the request, which must never be changed or omitted, that by grace, every 'intention, action and operation be directed purely to the praise and service of the Divine Majesty' [Exx. 46]. In the *Constitutions*, novices are told to 'strive' (*se ezfuerzen* [literally, 'force themselves']) for right intention both in regard to their vocation and in all details of life.[37] 'Right intention' in these texts means the God-directed intention, which Ignatius expresses in a variety of terms – 'praise', '*reverence', 'honour', '*service' and (most comprehensively) '*glory' – as distinct from an intention in which self-interest is primary and the place of God secondary. This understanding of right intention does not eclipse the distinction between ultimate intention and our immediate intentions, with their own immediate objectives and their sometimes complex subordinate relationships, but it relates every intention and every

---

[37] 'All should strive to keep their intention right', *Constitutions* Part III, c. 1, §1 [288] (Ganss, p. 165).

sequence of intentions to the one absolute end. Right intention, then, is the fundamental orientation of the will
towards God: into this orientation every immediate intention with its particular desired objective is subsumed.

Right intention is no preserve of the spirituality of
Ignatius. Certain particular concerns, however, lead
Ignatius to give emphasis to the subject and also to work
out his own way of understanding and approaching it.
Though concerned with intention across the total spectrum
of human freedom, his special concern is with that quality
of intentions that make up what is right – or not right – *for
me*, in a particular set of circumstances: decisions, attitudes, actions and patterns of activity, chosen situations and
relationships 'either morally indifferent or positively good
in themselves', cf [Exx. 170]. More particularly, the two
concerns mentioned above stand out: decision-making –
especially when the issue is the choice of a life-situation –
and the situations, relationships, and activities of the apostolic way of life The first is reflected in the *Exercises*, the
second in the *Constitutions* with their concern for right
intention in the 'love of creatures', study, and in general all
the concrete details of the living out of an apostolic vocation. Right intention is important in these two contexts not
only for the personal quality of the life of an individual, but
for the quality of the action and presence in the world of
the apostle.

Right intention is a *grace, and hence there can be
moments when we are graced to attain at a particular
moment and in a particular matter a singleness and integrity
of intention, as yet by no means habitual. Habitual right
intention, constant in our lives, cannot be achieved at a
stroke, nor indeed is it is ever achieved completely. Our
commitment is to grow towards it in a process requiring
effort ('striving') on our side, but an effort that takes place
within the action of the *Holy Spirit, which requires our
efforts but at the same time transcends them. The *Exercises*
contain an analysis of the content and dynamic of this
process, an analysis with relevance for the whole of life and

not simply for the well-defined issue of *election, which is the main concern of the *Exercises*. Certain questions about right intention are posed more acutely by the circumstances of daily life than in the *Exercises*; but it will be useful to begin with the latter before going on to some of the wider questions.

Intention in the Exercises

Basic to the *Exercises* is an understanding of the process by which right intention grows through dispositions, practical initiatives, and particular modes of *prayer. Four fundamental interrelated conditions are required, all gifts of grace but all calling for co-operative action on our part: the first is *vision*, the sense of the absoluteness of God; the second is the *desire springing from this, that the glory of God be the ultimate object to which the immediate objective of every specific intention is directed. Thus, what is immediately intended in the attitudes, thoughts or actions of daily life is intended as 'means' to the glory of God. But desire, however strongly felt, is ineffective without the *freedom* necessary for its implementation in the texture of everyday choices and actions. Freedom is an issue because the practical effectiveness of the desire for God is put in jeopardy by two potent related forces – the instinctive urge to keep control of one's life, and thus to try to relate to God without risk; and the compulsive attraction of our immediate *affections which seek to make absolutes of whatever for us constitute '*riches and honours'. This freedom again is the fruit of prayer, but at the same time it is something we on our side make efforts in the Spirit to promote, as, for example, when the exercitant takes the step of asking for the very contrary of the thing he or she feels compulsively attracted to by ill-ordered affection, drawing on freedom precisely in order to expand freedom against its opposite.

The fourth condition is *self-awareness*. This is crucial because of the defences and compromises which protect us from acknowledging the truth about ourselves. A helpful

feature of the *Exercises* as a pedagogy in right intention is
a series of examples of two kinds of situation:

> (i) the situation in which people evade the risk of a pure
> intention by effectively, but not explicitly, attaching
> God's will to their will, rather than theirs to God's will,
> while concealing from themselves that they are doing
> so;[38]
> (ii) the situation in which a seemingly right intention masks
> a 'real' intention of a quite different kind.[39]

Thus in the Three Classes, the exercitant considers the
cases of three people whose attachment to a fortune
acquired legitimately, but not for the love of God alone,
makes it difficult for them to ask what is the *will of God
candidly and with indifference, as right intention demands.
Asking the question could of course result in possession of
the goods precisely for the right intention, but could also
result in the loss of it. Right intention entails handing over
control to God. The risk of putting the question is considerable and the people of the First and Second Class avoid
it, in the first case by the compromise of procrastination, in
the second by the compromise of doing God's will having
first laid down the terms. In either case the control is
preserved which right intention hands over to God.

---

[38] Three Classes of persons: 'The persons of the second class would like
to be free of their attachment, but they want so to be free of it that they
retain the thing itself' [Exx. 154]; and in the Preamble to an Election,
'It often happens, for example, that people choose first of all to marry,
which is a means, and secondly to serve God in married life, though
the service of God is the end' [Exx. 169, and see 333].

[39] Directives for an Election, 3rd point: 'many deceive themselves,
making a divine vocation out of a biased or wrong election, whereas a
divine vocation is always pure and clear' [172]; and in the Rules for
Discernment, Second Set, one is warned that 'consolation can be given
by the good or bad angel', the latter so as to 'draw the person into
his own evil intention and wickedness' [Exx. 331].

Right intention in daily life

The Exercises are a school from which the exercitant returns to ordinary life to continue to 'strive for' the ideal that every intention, action and operation be directed to the praise, *reverence and *service of God. The main obstacle in this search, outside the Exercises as well as within them, is the ungenerosity, lack of trust and general weakness of fundamental *desire that the Exercises make us confront; and of course after the Exercises the exercitants carry into their forward journey all the resources for the formation of right intention that the Exercises have given them. But in ordinary life the search runs up also against situations and needs, which, though never absent, belong more to daily life than to the Exercises themselves with their particular focus and clarity. More than in the Exercises themselves one runs up against obstacles coming from the multi-layered complexity of mind, will, and emotion: the limitations of freedom; the opacity of self-knowledge; the frequent uncertainty as to the real reasons for our actions and reactions; the power of defences that do not quickly yield even to discernment; the interweaving of our own intentions and defences with the intentions and defences of our milieu.

This situation tends to evoke one of two antithetical responses: on the one hand virtually to limit serious consideration of right intention to major issues only, on the other to try to live in a state of constant, and for the most part anxious, self-scrutiny. Both responses downplay the truth that growth in right intention is primarily the work of the *Holy Spirit. The fact that we have the Spirit means that we have a *desire for God not of our own making, and that the thrust of the action of the Spirit is to intensify our desire, and bring into line with it all the complex elements of human motivation, including the unconscious itself. Our own efforts or striving are feasible only when they consist first and foremost in yielding to this action. Our co-operation with the Spirit carries, however, certain practical implications, and it benefits from a sense of the main blocks and misunderstandings that can stand in its way. In this connection the following should especially be noted.

Intention and context

First, the authentic continuing development of right intention is intrinsically connected with the authentic development of the faith-vision which is its context. Good intentions and defective vision make a notoriously disastrous marriage, and part of the function of the *Exercises* is to draw in broad strokes the theological background necessary for rightly intentioned *election. The vision progressively built up in the various stages of making the Exercises is therefore essential to their purpose of enabling an election to be made on the basis of 'right intention'. Though, however, the vision proposed in the Exercises is for life, this does not mean that it is static and final. Even in the time of the Exercises themselves, and certainly in the tensions between tradition and change inherited by the incipient twenty-first century, faith-vision must necessarily be in a state of constant development. The development of authentic vision is both a subjective and an objective process. As subjective, it requires discernment and freedom: the *discernment* that senses the authentic and the inauthentic in the very reactions of *consolation and desolation; the *freedom* to be listeners to God's ongoing word, objectively open to all the ways in which in the Church and in one's own Christian community a faith-vision is being continually formed.

Intention and desire

The basis, the essential motivational force of right intention, is the *desire* to live by, and surrender oneself to, God. Only this desire makes a person free enough to see things in relation to God and his will, and to overcome a natural reluctance to relinquish self-interest. In ordinary life, therefore, as in the Exercises, the first condition for the extension of right intention into the details of life, and into the resistant layers of the psyche, is that the heart become increasingly pervaded by the *desire for God.

Intention and consciousness

It is important to maintain a balance in one's attitudes towards right intention in relation to *self-knowledge*.

On the one hand self-knowledge, both spiritual and psychological, is essential. There can be no pursuit of right intention without discernment, the growing ability to sense the movements of spiritual consonance and dissonance in consciousness; but there is also need for a high measure of natural self-awareness and self-candour, the capability, at least on reflection and perhaps with help, of 'getting in touch' with feelings and reactions below the immediate surface of awareness, and of recognizing the defences by which we can hide from ourselves.

On the other hand, there are dangers in identifying right intention too closely with *consciousness*. For all Ignatius' insistence on habitual discernment and his expectations regarding the moments of *election in the Exercises, right intention does not imply continual consciousness of the spiritual quality, act by act, of present motivation. In this matter, most of the time at any rate, complete lucidity is not given to us:

> Very few persons in this life – and to press the point, I would say nobody – can calculate and form an appraisal of the degree to which they impede and undo the effectiveness of the Lord's influence on themselves.[40]

As for psychological insight into ourselves, vital as this is, the rightness of intention at a given moment is not measured by one's capacity for introspection, nor by one's

---

[40] Ignatius of Loyola, letter to Francis Borgia, late in 1545 (no. 101: MHSI ed., I, 339–342), *Personal Writings*, p. 161.

insights into the ways of the mind. Moreover, though right intention in any activity requires a habitual prayerfulness coming frequently, if briefly, into focus, in much rightly intentioned activity the object of consciousness is not God and his will, but the task to which one believes God's will commits one. In general, too much dependency on experiential evidence of right intention takes the emphasis away from two things: that right intention is a *habitual* orientation of will that persists through changing modes and foci of consciousness; and that the basis of this orientation is the influence of the *Holy Spirit within us. In co-operating with the Spirit the first focus must be on trust in, and surrender to, the Spirit.

Right intention and study

Ignatius is specially concerned with intention in *study*, on which he sets the highest value: as the *Constitutions* observe, study absorbs the whole person: '... their devoting themselves to learning, which they acquire with a pure intention of serving God and which in a certain way requires the whole man, will be not less, but rather more pleasing to God our Lord during the time of study'.[41] There should be no half-measures, therefore, in the Jesuit's commitment to study. Jesuit scholastics are to be 'thoroughly genuine and earnest students' and be protected in their study from every possible distraction.[42] While absorbed in study the spirit could always 'grow cool in their love of true virtues and of *religious life'.[43] Study requires, therefore, that the students seek in their studies nothing but the *glory of God and the good of souls, and it has the value Ignatius accords to it only in so far as the student's intention is of this quality. Hence the practices he suggests to maintain right intention: given that only limited time is

41 *Constitutions*, Part 4, ch. 4, §2 [340], ed. Ganss, p. 183.
42 Ibid., ch. 6, §2 [361], ed. Ganss, p. 190.
43 Ibid., Part 4, ch. 4, §2 [340], ed. Ganss, p. 183.

available for specifically religious practices (the 'normal'
exercises for scholastics are 'the daily Mass, an hour for
recitation [of the Little Office] and *examen of conscience,
and confession and communion once a week'), 'they can try
to practise a constant seeking of Our Lord in all things: e.g.
when talking to someone, or walking, or looking around,
when enjoying some taste, or listening, or trying to understand ...'[44]

Right intention and psychology

In view of all this it may be asked what is the relationship
of the spiritual concepts of right and disordered intention
with the motivations connected with the unconscious, or at
any rate with the unacknowledged needs, *fears, and
defences often discovered with the help of psychology. It
should be noted that right intention is not a psychological
concept, but a theocentric one with psychological implications – a basic orientation of will not immediately towards
psychological integrity but to the *glory of God. As this
orientation develops it will tend to bring into line with
itself every dynamism – even unconscious – that might
influence attitudes or behaviour. But at any given moment
right intention operates within our *de facto* freedom and
self-knowledge, and hence at any given moment right intention is consistent with 'hidden agendas'. But it is not
compatible with a closure of the mind, with any attitude
that constitutes a refusal – to listen to the ever-fresh word
of God and to be open to the light which is forever illumi-
nating reality in new ways.

---

44   In 1551, in reply to a series of questions raised by a Portuguese scholas-
     tic, Fr Antonio Brandao, Ignatius commissioned Polanco to draw up a
     memo with appropriate answers: Letter no. 1854, MHSI III 506–513,
     cf. *Inigo: Letters Personal and Spiritual*, Letter 38, 'Problems of Young
     Candidates', p. 177.

Ultimate intention and immediate meaning

As with *love and *desire the language of Ignatius regarding intention can leave an impression that his insistent focus on the reality of God must detract from the consistency and meaningfulness of immediate reality – the things, the persons, the tasks of daily life, above all the tasks and commitments of personal relationships.

In reply, firstly, Ignatius wants to leave no doubt of the *challenge* that the affective integrity of right intention raises to instinct-based values and experiences. But, secondly, while not playing down this challenge we should be aware of some of the ways in which it can be misunderstood: '*all things' in Ignatius' terminology implies the reality and consistency that things have in themselves – specifically, our loves, our interests, and our commitments. Moreover, God-directed intention does not mean that we must always be thinking about God, at least in the sense of our explicitly thinking about God (as distinct from his being a presence and a background). Ignatius recognizes this when he speaks of study as absorbing the 'whole' person. God-centred intention does not imply the elimination of other intentions, but the integration of all immediate intentions into our ultimate intention, and in this process their purification of every element incompatible, in however slight a degree, with an existence focussed wholly on God and his *will. In the end we must remember that any attempt to interpret Ignatius experientially must recognize that it is the Spirit who gives integration to our intentions, and that the experience of such integration may not be easily imaginable to people who have not embarked on the journey.

God is the creator of every layer and process of the human psyche. But given the desire for growth, the rightness of intention at a given moment is not measured by one's capacity for introspection, nor by one's insights into the ways of the mind, but by the strength of the *desire to follow the Spirit. If this desire is authentic it will include the willingness to take every means to collaborate in the processes by which the Spirit extends freedom and discernment into the unfree and obscure areas of the self. If the intention of the Spirit purifies us radically of even the subtlest forms of egocentricity, such as self-satisfaction in desiring God's work, it must not be thought that God, as ultimate meaning, is the enemy of immediate meanings, or that the drives that enable us to undertake specific tasks (e.g. interest) are necessarily selfish. Since it a process of the Spirit it expands possibilities, but does so at the pace of the grace given to each. Hence, the collaboration on our part must be both serious and also patient.

Love

Love is the subject of many texts in the *Exercises* where there is no mention of the word 'love'. The opening sentence of the Foundation, for instance is about love, which people of Ignatius' day would have found it natural to describe, even outside of a religious context, in terms such as 'praise, *reverence and *service'.[45] In the four Weeks, love appears first in the form of 'mercy' – specially needed as such by a person in the situation evoked in the second Prelude of the first Meditation [Exx. 48]. 'Love', named as such, first appears in the fifth Meditation (on Hell) with the statement that it is the love of the eternal Lord that keeps us on the moral path, though, should it grow weak, it may need the reinforcement of *fear. Love,

---

[45] See, for example, Ignatius' account of his day-dreams, while convalescing: 'what he was to do in the service of a certain lady...', *Personal Writings*, 'Reminiscences', §6, pp. 14–15.

then, is presented from the outset as it is defined in the
Contemplatio, as consisting not of words but actions – here,
the actions of a converted life. This principle is basic to the
use of the word 'love' in the sense of 'love of God' (ours
for God, or God's for us) in the *Exercises* – love in the
Exercises is either an élan towards action or the best affective context for discernment, never simply an end-point.
This does not mean of course that a person who 'finds' the
experience of love will not rest in it without immediately
'wanting to move on', but if the experience is authentic, its
*inner momentum will quickly assert itself – as love
leading to *service*.

The texts that refer specifically to love have a double
interest: they illustrate a consistent and distinctively Ignatian emphasis, and they lead us to explore the relation
between the two objects of love, God and *creatures.
Ignatius' doctrine on love revolves around these two loves
and the relationship between them: the love of God (God's
for us and ours for God) and the entire range of our loves
for created things.

The love of God

In *God's love for us*, the characteristics of love pinpointed
in the C*ontemplatio* – love consists in deeds rather than
words, and in giving whatever one has or is able to give
[Exx. 231] – are fully realized. God's love shows itself not
only in words (notably those of the prophets and of Jesus),
but in the reality those words disclose and interpret: the
action of God and his sharing of himself with his creature
as far as the nature of God and creature allows. God's love
is a constant self-giving activity at the heart of all created
reality, and especially in the lives of people. It is this self-
giving activity that the exercitant contemplates under
various aspects in the four points of the *Contemplatio* [Exx.
234–237]. The same self-giving activity is the source of the
stirring and enlightenment deep within our experience, pre-
supposed by the discernment rules.

In *our love for God* we respond to the initiative of God who first loves us. Our response consists fundamentally in an assent, a 'yes' to this love, an assent which may consist either in yielding ourselves to a love experienced in *consolation, or in an act of faith in a love not for the moment reflected in feelings (cf. the insistence on God's love in a letter written by Ignatius to a dispirited Teresa Rejadell[46]). But assent to God's love is not just a matter of passivity; it takes God's way of loving as model. Our love for God is authentic, then, to the extent to which it works out in self-gift and in the actions and choices of service. No authentic Christian tradition denies, of course, the connection between love, *service, and self-gift: separated from these, love would be a velleity. But if the connection is implicit in any authentic understanding of love, Ignatius stands out for the insistence with which he makes the implicit explicit, so much so that in the text of the *Exercises* the term 'love' never appears except as in some way related to service. In the Four Weeks, the word 'love' makes its first appearance in the *Exercises* as the ordinary motive for fidelity to the *will of God [Exx. 65]. In the Kingdom exercise, 'those moved by love ' [Exx. 97] are precisely those who wish also to be outstanding in service. The petition of the Second Week asks for the grace of a love that leads to following, or discipleship [Exx. 104]. The request of the *Contemplatio* is for the grace in everything to love God and also to serve him [Exx. 233], and the self-offering, 'Take, Lord, and receive', is the prayer of a person strongly moved by love, *afectándose mucho* ['with heartfelt love' Exx. 234]. Where decisions are concerned, not only must the love of God be their motive [Exx. 150, 184, 338], but decisions are ideally made in an experience of *consolation, in which one feels 'inflamed' with the love of God [Exx. 15]. An authentic experience of loving God contains, therefore, an *élan* to service and self-giving, and gives rise to an enlightenment of the mind which is the best disposition in which to make choices.

[46] *Personal Writings*, letter 4 (no. 7: I, 99–107), pp. 129–35.

Our loves for created things

Ignatius uses the language of love both of personal relationships and of attachments to other realities than people,
e.g. *riches, fame, ecclesiastical or secular office, a
benefice, 'fame' or its opposite [Exx. 23]. In the *Exercises*
the distinction between these is not always made explicit;
sometimes the reference is clearly non-personal [e.g. Exx.
316], but in many cases the readers themselves are left to
make their own application of a general concept. Only in
the 'Rules for Almsgiving' [Exx. 338] is love referred
unambiguously to persons. The two loves are not however
of the same kind, and Ignatius' habit of lumping 'creatures'
together without further differentiation does not mean that
he himself played down the distinctiveness of personal love.
The love (whether disordered or ordered) that one might
feel towards a benefice is not the love (whether ordered or
disordered) that one might experience towards a person,
which at its most true consists in desire for and pleasure
in another's good, expressed through sharing and self-
commitment.

Love of any kind, however, is an 'affection' – a *desire,
attachment and, indeed, need of the heart; and as such all
loves are subject to the principles of affective conversion
which are basic to the *Exercises*. The concern of the *Exercises* is to bring the exercitants to a mutually endorsing
integration of the loves of God and creatures by taking them
through the stages of affective conversion. An authentic
relationship to any creature requires 'right *intention',
freedom (or '*indifference') in the search for God's will. It
requires that whatever may be immature, or self-interested,
or 'unfree' in a person's attachments, be relinquished or
transcended, and that the style and very situation of our
use-of-creatures relationships be such as to conduce to 'the
praise, reverence and service of God our Lord'. He insists
also that one creature can only authentically love another
creature in relation to the love in which each is held by the
Creator and Lord of each. The conditions for authentic love

require, then, a 'Second Week person', one committed to
the radical following of Christ.

Where these conditions are accepted, a person can grow
towards a disposition, perhaps inconstant at first, but eventually a habitual climate, in which love of God and of
creature come together in a lived synthesis. There are two
keys to this synthesis: first, authentic love or desire for
'creatures' has its *source* in God; thus in the *Exercises*
(once in an unspecified context [Exx. 184, but cf Exx. 178]
and once in connection with relatives or friends [Exx.
338]), he refers to a love or desire for a creature which is
somehow sensed as descending from above and in which
God shines forth. Second, when our love or desire for creatures is of this kind, participating in the love or the desire
of God himself, then God is also 'in' the *object* of our love
in such a way that in a love for another we love God, and
in our love for God we love the one we love. The *Constitutions* urge that the companions be frequently exhorted to
such a love. The first of the three kinds of *consolation is
described as an experience in which to love a creature
except in relation to God is impossible [Exx. 316].

A question

Ignatius' main concern is how to integrate our loves into
our love of God in a way that in no way diminishes the total
quality of the latter. But he asks the question from a conviction that *grace does not destroy but builds on nature, and
hence he implies that the love by which we love 'in Christ',
while purified and changed – indeed transformed – by and
with our being graced, is not destroyed but made truly
itself. Today, however, our concern is with love as *experience*, and we ask more urgently than Ignatius did, how our
loves 'in God' have the emotional quality constitutive of
human love.

Do Ignatius' principles express a spirituality in which our
natural *affections are transformed and raised by grace, or
one in which they are seen as the enemies of grace and to

be suppressed? There are many reasons for this latter impression, the first among them being that love is a subject on which we are considerably more willing to challenge the classic spiritual masters of the spiritual life than to be challenged by them.

The theme of divine and human loves in synthesis is one of the more important ways in which Ignatius speaks to the spiritual needs of our own age. Its force, however, can be weakened by an impression that for all its immediate promise Ignatius' concept of an intregrated love is less than it appears at first sight, that he seems to describe a love to some degree diminished – deprived of something of its human quality – precisely by its integration into the love of God. The impression comes partly from the very *language* of well-known Ignatian texts, partly from a widespread lack of familiarity with the *wider reach of Ignatius writings*, partly from the fact that love is a subject on which the *language of one age* can differ very much from that of another.

On the *language*, the reader is referred to the comments on *affections and right *intention. Here two particular points need to be made. Loving a creature for itself, when distinguished from loving it *in* (or for the sake of) God means loving a creature in such a way as effectively to deny the relationship with God in which it is grounded, and hence to love *in*authentically. And the famous text which insists that kindred are to be given 'only that love which rightly ordered charity requires'[47] is addressed to a candidate for the Society of Jesus, presumed by Ignatius to be still emotionally bound by the powerful family ties of kinship characteristic of his time.[48]

---

[47] *General Examen of Candidates*, ch. 4, §7 (tr., Ganss, p. 95).

[48] [English translations of the *Exercises* [316] tend to use the word 'only' to convey the Spanish *sino* in the phrase, *ninguna cosa ... puede amar ... sino en el Criador y Señor de todas ellas*; but Ivens preferred 'if not'; he explains his reason, based on the Latin versions: 'the point is the wholly positive one that there is a grace of consolation in which the experience of loving God takes all other lovers into itself', *Understanding the Spiritual Exercises*, p. 215.]

But even when misreadings of the more analytic texts are
obviated, it remains true that these texts, with their conci-
sion and their preoccupation with distinctions and
connections, convey little of the empirical feel of integrated
love. To find this in Ignatian sources one must turn to his
life and letters. But it must be remembered too that human
relations are an area particularly subject to the variations in
culture, and it is for us to go on formulating our own ways
of expressing Ignatius' essential insight. In this connection,
a person today seeking to formulate the integration of
divine and human loves might find inspiration in Bonhoeffer's image of the two loves as forming part of the
'polyphony of life':

> There is always a danger of intense love destroying what I
> might call the 'polyphony' of life. What I mean is that God
> requires that we should love him eternally with our whole
> hearts, yet not so as to compromise or diminish our earthly
> affections, but as a kind of *cantus firmus* to which the other
> melodies of life provide the counterpoint ... Where the
> ground bass is firm and clear, there is nothing to stop the
> counterpoint from being developed to the utmost of its limits.
> Both ground bass and counterpoint are 'without confusion and
> yet distinct', in the words of the Chalcedonian formula, like
> Christ in his divine and human natures.
>
> (*Letters and Papers from Prison*, 19 May, 1944,
> pp. 99–100)[49]

---

[49] [For the text of the definition of Chalcedon, cf. Tanner, *Decrees*, vol.
1, p. 86.]

Mortal sin

The term *pecado mortal* can refer in the *Exercises* either to
the seven capital sins, or to 'mortal sin' in the sense in
which an action may be 'mortal' as opposed to 'venial', the
sense intended being sometimes clear and sometimes
ambiguous.

The Church from earliest times has declared certain
actions to constitute in themselves 'matter' for mortal sin,
though mortal sin consists not in an action in itself, but an
action issuing from freedom and judgement. In the early
Church the declared 'mortal sins' were three, viz. homi-
cide, adultery, and apostasy. Over the centuries
specifications of grave matter increased considerably,
possibly with a resulting legalism (with attendant anxiety
and scrupulosity) and a loss of the spiritual sense of grave
sin.

Behind the term 'mortal sin', in the second sense, is the
principle that it is possible for a human action to have the
quality of total and free decision of the whole person
against God or his *will. Such a decision (which is reversed
in *repentance*) is a decision for death (the sins both of the
angels and of Eve and Adam were of this kind [Exx.
50–51]). The ordinary sinful actions of human beings do
not have the totality of a 'mortal' sin and are called
'venial'.

Ignatius probably subscribed to the common view of his
time that mortal sin was of frequent occurrence in the lives
of ordinarily mediocre Christians. It should be noted,
however, that the First Week exercises nowhere refer to the
'mortal sins' of the exercitant, but only to 'numerous' and
'capital' sins.

Pride

Pride is a stance of the will, which implicitly or explicitly denies one's need for, and dependency on, God; it asserts self against the ground of self. To be proud is to seek to replace God by 'self' as the centre of one's personal universe. Pride is, therefore, the fundamental sin. It is also the fundamental temptation. With maturity, the temptation does not cease, but conceals itself under increasingly subtle forms: integral to every temptation to pride is the search for ways of sustaining and boosting the egocentric self.

Basic to the *Exercises* is the thesis that in dealing with Second Week exercitants (presumed to be in the Illuminative Way) the main strategy of the '*enemy of human nature' [Exx. 7, 10, 135, 325–327, 334] is to nurture pride by arousing covetous desire for *riches and honours. Between the deadly sin of pride and these desires there is an intrinsic link. The key to this link is to be found in the complex and deep significance in human life of such realities as possessions, power, success and status. More than bringing immediate gratifications, these have to do with the very development of the self, with identity, with being somebody as distinct from being nobody. Precisely because property and positions have the effect of building the sense of *self*, they can build the perverted sense of self that constitutes pride. That we are affirmed as free individual beings in the world by the immediate realities described as riches and honours [Exx. 142] is not only, however, the key to the dynamics of pride. It is also the basis of Ignatius' understanding of *humility. But the humble person relates to the world on the basis of a search for the *will of God in spiritual freedom, and for such a person the affirmations that come from immediate realities mediate the affirmation of God himself. The proud person, on the other hand, uses immediate affirmations as screens against the claims of God – and also against recognizing the real consequences of isolation from God ('For you say, I am rich, I have prospered, and I need nothing, not knowing that you are wretched, pitiable, poor, blind, and naked', Revelation 3:17).

To appreciate and apply to one's own situation the
'*riches-honours-pride' strategy, three points need especially to be noted:

1. The Tempter of the Two Standards is specified as Lucifer,
   the fallen angel of light, who tempts through the plausible.
   Pride, the object, is incurred without being named. Even
   where the first steps, 'wealth . . . honours' [Exx. 142], are
   concerned, there is no question of anything objectively
   wrong (e.g., the acquisition of riches by dishonest means).
   The wealth and honours of the Two Standards, like the
   fortune of the Three Classes of persons, are legitimate in
   themselves. This being so, the fact that in a particular case
   they might be 'vain', even indeed the craving and dependency that constitute covetousness, may seem to the
   unsuspecting to be matters of no great importance, even if
   they are noticed.
2. Pride takes many shapes: as a relation to God, it sometimes
   takes the form of forgetfulness of God, sometimes of
   making God the ever-present backer-up of the *ego*, the God
   who is always on my side. Among the ways pride is
   embodied in relations to self, others, and the world, the
   social pride based on wealth, power and prestige might be
   described as 'typical pride' (as being without possessions is
   typical *poverty). But pride takes other forms too.
   Comparative freedom from typical pride in no way implies
   freedom from essentially proud attitudes. Hence for some
   people, it is important to find where their own pride lies;
   and it should be noted that some people do not need to have
   pride explained in a way that would associate pride with
   healthy assertiveness. Moreover, pride often refers simply
   to basic dignity or a satisfaction in achievement (as in the
   line of the hymn: 'We shall guard each man's dignity, and
   save each man's pride').
3. *Riches and honour cover many realities. In the sixteenth
   century 'riches' would have suggested to an exercitant a
   fortune, a well-endowed benefice, or a lucrative office;
   'honours' would suggest the social or ecclesiastical power
   or prestige that spring from prosperity and position. The
   equivalents today constitute the central challenge of secular
   culture to the Gospel. In interpreting riches and honour, as

in interpreting 'actual poverty', it is important not to play down the immediate material and social situations suggested by the terms; but without playing down the literal understanding of the *enemy programme, it is important to recognize the wider range of riches. The notion covers such realities as achievements, talents, projects, ideas, relationships – anything in the end which affirms, gives us a sense of worth, and which we can easily desire, cling to, depend upon, for our happiness, security, or self-importance.

The capital sin of pride consists essentially in making oneself equal to God – in the denial of God's lordship over oneself. In essence, therefore, as an attitude towards God it expresses itself in a wide range of attitudes and forms of behaviour that might be called social pride, calculated to affirm oneself by affirming one's superiority over others. There is an essential two-way connection between pride, in its direct relationship to God, and what can be termed social pride; hence the standard wisdom subscribed to by Ignatius, which sees every assault on social pride as an assault on pride in its spiritual essence.

Profit/Profitable

These terms[50] are to be understood in relation to another fundamental theme of the *Exercises*, *desire. The exercitant is presumed to desire the twofold purpose of the *Exercises*:

[50] Very frequently used in the *Exercises* (at least thirty references in the Concordances, see Echarte, or Teinonen), usually in the verbal form, *aprovechar*, 'to be good for one' (in modern Castilian, *¡qué aproveche!* is like the French, *bon appétit!*).

spiritual freedom and finding the will of God. It is presumed that such a person desire the specific '*grace' of the exercise currently being made, and is aware of particular and personal needs and desires which arise as the exercises go on. What *profits*, then, is what helps towards the realization of these desires.

One-sided preoccupation with *profit* could lead to a calculating and over-anxious attitude. Rightly understood, however, the terms recall the fact that the options of the exercitant are governed by the basic rule of the Foundation, that what 'helps' is to be done, and what does not help is to be avoided [Exx. 23], and hence the need for self-awareness, seriousness, and purposiveness in our own co-operation with the *Holy Spirit.

The *profit* criterion also helps to preserve the exercitant from straying into interpretations or applications of the *Exercises*, even from seeking realms of experience, which here-and-now would distract from the path on which he or she is being led by the deep desires of the Spirit.

Reverence

To give reverence to God is one of the purposes for which the free creature, whether the human person [Exx. 23] or the angel [Exx. 50], is made. The term can be defined as 'respect for another', inspired precisely by their irreducible otherness. An essential component of all authentic *love, reverence is the guarantee that the other is loved for themselves, and their protection against being made into a possession. Applied to our relationship to God, *reverence* is the attitude inspired by the ontological difference between the infinite and the finite, between creator and creature. The person who loves God reverentially – and God can be loved authentically in no other way – loves God precisely *as God* and will never try to possess God.

Reverence, both for God and people, is a constant of Christian life, a defining characteristic of authentic quality. But the *Exercises* together with other Ignatian texts illustrate that it also admits of a wide diversity of focus, experience, and practical expressions. Thus while reverence consists essentially in an attitude, there are moments when it is especially appropriate to express reverence in a particular bodily act [Exx. 75]. There are also situations where reverence as an attitude needs to be made deliberately explicit, for instance, situations which in themselves call especially for reverence (e.g. the transition into a more contemplative mode of *prayer [Exx. 3]), or in which the need for reverence is easily overlooked (e.g. oath-taking [Exx. 38]). Moreover, while there is a level at which we can choose or elicit reverence, there are Spirit-given movements of reverence which we can in no way attain by our own powers; such movements, usually accompanied by intense feeling, are described frequently in the *Spiritual Diary*. Ignatius recognizes that reverence has a loving and a *fearful mode. Fear-reverence can have its place, but the reverence which is a typical motif of Ignatian spirituality is a way of loving.

While the basis of all reverence is the reverence for God, the reverence owed to God is extended to God's creatures, who in various ways represent God. The idealized earthly king receives reverence from all princes [Exx. 92]. In the *Constitutions* the principle of reverencing God through people is central to Ignatius' position on authority, and the linking of *love and reverence in a single phrase is characteristic of texts dealing with subject-superior relationships. But reverence does not require hierarchy; it belongs also to the familiar and equal relationships of one Jesuit to another.

Finally, neither the experience nor the expression of

reverence are in any way obstructed by the mean, the undignified, the unglamorous. Indeed with reverence, as with *glory, Ignatius likes to juxtapose a sublime religious concept with the harsher aspects of *service. However, there are problems about reverence in an age which is considerably less formal than was, at least at first sight, that of Ignatius. For Ignatius reverence towards those in authority or to possessors of social rank was culturally connatural; for evidence one need only note the distinctive tone of his correspondence with Francis Borgia.[51] We can readily understand therefore that reverence for God came naturally to Ignatius, but might ask whether reverence should have the same place in the spirituality of our more egalitarian age. We need to look beyond particular cultural expressions of reverence to the essence of reverence as a factor in relationships, and remember that for Ignatius to show reverence was a positive experience.

Vainglory

As the object of rightly intentioned acts is the *glory of God, so the attitude of vainglory is the glory of self; and as the glory of God is God's presence, in such a way as to draw praise and *reverence, so the object of vainglory is that the presence of self should win, in a literal sense or otherwise, praise and reverence. The term is always used of actions which are otherwise morally neutral or even in

For some examples, cf. *Personal Writings*, Letters 13 (No. 101, I, 339–42), 21 (No. 466, II, 233–7), 22 (No. 790, II, 494–5), pp. 160–3, 204–9.

themselves positively good.[52] Vainglory is used by the
*enemy at two levels, corresponding roughly to levels of
spiritual maturity. At one level the temptation is to simple
self-aggrandisement in the esteem one has aroused in
another or others. Ignatius recognized such a possibility in
giving the complete answer when a lady from whom he
begged alms in Spain asked where he was going. Had he
admitted he was going to Jerusalem he would have made an
impression that would have caused him to experience the
egocentric satisfaction of vainglory.

But with spiritual maturity a more subtle temptation
occurs which can prove particularly insidious in its consequences for an apostle, namely the temptation not to do
something good because by doing so one might incur vainglory.

52 Cf. Thomas Becket's remark in T. S. Eliot's *Murder in the Cathedral*:
'The last temptation is the greatest treason / To do the right deed for the
wrong reason', T. S. Eliot, *Collected Plays*, London (Faber & Faber),
1962, p. 30.

Part IV

In Memory
of Michael Ivens

§1 Biography and Publications

Joseph A. Munitiz, SJ

10 Feb. 1933 born in Upminster, Essex; baptized Michael Haworth (his mother's maiden name); his father worked as manager of Securities in the Midland Bank; education at St Ignatius, Stamford Hill

7 Sept. 1951 joined the Society of Jesus at Harlaxton Manor, near Grantham

8 Sept. 1953 First Vows, and move to Roehampton; Juniorate (humanities)

1954–1956 two years of scholastic philosophy at Heythrop College (Oxon.)

1956–1958 third year of philosophy and teacher training at Roehampton

1958–1961 history degree at Campion Hall, Oxford

1961–1963 teaching at Stonyhurst (history and French)

1963–1967 theology at Lyon; long essay on Jean-Joseph Surin, SJ, ordination to the priesthood in 1966

1967–1968 tertianship at St Beuno's with Fr Paul Kennedy as Instructor

1968–1969 assistant chaplain at Manchester University

1969–1971 'spiritual father' [chaplain] at Campion Hall; assitant editor of *The Way*

1971 move to Old Windsor; assistant to Fr James Walsh

1972–1976 ditto, but in Southwell House, London; numerous articles; starts work on book on Ignatius; absences to conduct three-month

	Tertianships for Brothers in Sunderland (1972), Australia (1974), and Rhodesian [now Zimbabwe] Mission (1975)
1976–2005	move to St Beuno's as Tertian Instructor; later member of the team running the Spirituality Centre, almost until his death; work on publications; brain surgery 1990 (see §5)
9 Sept. 2005	death

Publications

Unpublished Writings

1. 'The spiritual doctrine of Jean-Joseph Surin' [65 pages], Long Essay (*opus scientificum*) written to qualify for his theological degree at the Jesuit theological Faculty, Lyon, 1967 [with critical judgement by F. Courel, SJ].
2. 'The idea of the lay vocation in Francis de Sales' [25 pages], probably essay written while in Theology.
3. *Discernment* [23 pages, talk, photocopied for distribution], not dated.
4. [Translation] Francesc Riera, SJ, *The Exercises in Ordinary Life* [for private use], 38 pages, not dated.
5. Typescripts of various talks remain among the papers.

Books

Understanding the Spiritual Exercises: Text and Commentary: A Handbook for Retreat Directors [Inigo Texts

Series: 4], Leominster, Gracewing and Inigo Enterprises, 1998.

[Translation] Javier Melloni, SJ, *The Exercises of St Ignatius Loyola in the Western Tradition* [Inigo Texts Series: 5] Leominster, Gracewing and Inigo Enterprises, 2000.

— [Translation] *The Spiritual Exercises of Saint Ignatius of Loyola*, with an Introduction by Gerard W. Hughes, SJ, [Inigo Texts Series: 8], Leominster, Gracewing and Inigo Enterprises, 2004.

Articles

'The Crucified Church', *The Way*, January 1969, pp. 12–20.

'Old and New', *The Way*, October 1969, pp. 292–301.

'Religious Poverty in contemporary writing', *The Way Supplement*, 9, 1970 (Spring), pp. 75–86.

'Celibacy in contemporary writing', *The Way Supplement*, 10, 1970 (Summer), pp. 98–116.

— 'Salvation: Confidence or Anxiety', *The Way*, October 1970, pp. 327–35.

'Liturgy of Consecration', *The Way Supplement*, 11, 1971 (Spring), pp. 47–58.

'Temptations against Faith', *The Way*, July 1971, pp. 226–34.

'Ministry and secularity', *The Way Supplement* 13, 1971 (Summer), pp. 45–57.

'The Dimension of Group Prayer', *The Way Supplement* 16, 1972 (Summer), pp. 67–79.

— 'What Should I be?' *The Way*, October 1972, pp. 263–74.

'Progress in Values', *The Way*, April 1973, pp. 126–36.

— 'Pentecostal Prayer' [with Edmund Colledge, OSA, in the section 'When you pray'], *The Way*, October 1973, pp. 325–36.

'Planning Tomorrow's Ministry', *The Way Supplement* 23, 1974 (Autumn), pp. 43–54.

— 'The Rhythm of Prayer and Action', *The Way Supplement* 28, 1976 (Summer), pp. 20-9.

✓— 'Healing the Divided Self', *The Way*, July 1976, pp. 163–75.

'My experience as a parishioner, 1933–1951', *St Joseph's, Upminster, Parish Newsletter*, prob. *c*.1980.

'The Eighteenth Annotation and the Early Directories', *The Way Supplement* 46, 1983 (Spring), pp. 3-10.

— 'The First Week: Some Notes on the Text', *The Way Supplement* 48, 1983 (Autumn), pp. 3-14.

'Homily preached on the occasion of the funeral of Fr James Walsh, 25 February, 1986, at St Beuno's', *Letters and Notices*, 87 (391), Christmas 1986, pp. 201-8.

— 'Finding God in all things – the spirituality of everyday life', *Stonyhurst Magazine*, 485, 1988, pp. 13–16.

'Poverty in the *Constitutions* and Other Ignatian Sources', *The Way Supplement* 61, 1988 (Spring), pp. 76-88.

— 'Desire and Discernment', *The Way Supplement* 95, 1999 (Summer), pp. 31-43.

§2 Congratulatory Letter[1] for the Golden Jubilee of Fr Michael Ivens' Entry into the Society of Jesus

Peter-Hans Kolvenbach, SJ,
Superior General of the Society of Jesus

Curia Generalizia della Compagnia di Gesù
Borgo S. Spirito, 4
C.P. 6139 / 00195 ROMA-PRAITI (Italia)
                                              7 September 2001
Dear Father Ivens, P.C.

With great pleasure I offer you my heartfelt congratulations on your fifty years as a Jesuit. It is in the spirit of Ignatian service that these years are called 'golden' because they are a precious gift of God. I join you in thanking Him for that gift, for the countless moments of grace that first enabled you to respond to His call and that have kept you faithful to that commitment for over half a century. In the midst of a world that does not understand the value of a lifelong commitment, your fifty years of generous fidelity are an effective witness to the continuing presence of God in our lives today.

You have always had a gift for friendship. A wide variety of people you have known continue to keep in touch

---

[1] [It is customary for the Superior General of the Jesuits to write and congratulate each Jesuit on the Golden Jubilee of his entry; the letter sent to Michael Ivens in 2001 is reproduced here, with kind permission of Fr General. It gives an idea of the esteem in which he was held among his fellow Jesuits.]

with you and to inquire after you, a sign of the love and esteem you inspire. It is noticeable that when decisions are under discussion you ensure that personal considerations and human values are not overlooked. Compassion always weighs heavily with you.

Among the fifteen or so members of the resident community at St Beuno's, your presence is truly valued, your gentle influence always significant and your judgement very highly respected. You wear your great learning lightly and humbly, and you have a delightful sense of humour. You are sincerely welcoming to visitors and considerate of their needs.

Your immensely impressive book, *Understanding the Spiritual Exercises*, shows that learning on such a vital subject can be expressed with clarity and in a felicitous style. Not surprisingly you have been, and continue to be, highly esteemed as a spiritual director to many Jesuits and to others. For many years you did an outstanding job as tertian-master. Your judgement in spiritual and theological matters is of a high order and always carries conviction.

For the last ten years you have had to bear continual difficulties of health; but you have done so always with very edifying patience and even humour. Without you St Bueno's would be lacking a good deal of its 'heart' and 'soul'.

I join your many friends in wishing you the full joy of this jubilee day, praying that your ministry continue to give both you and them much consolation and joy in your Jesuit vocation. To mark this occasion, then, I gladly assign, from the treasury of the Society, fifty Masses for your intentions. Please remember me and the needs of the Society in your own prayers and sacrifices.

Sincerely in Christ,
Peter-Hans Kolvenbach, SJ,
Superior General

§3 The *Way* Community

Michael Ivens, SJ

These notes and reflections originate in my last general
Christmas letter, in which I mentioned that on account of
my blindness I would now almost certainly never complete
the book I was writing, 'During and Out of the *Way*
Community Experience'. The book would have been a
general survey of the themes of Ignatian spirituality on
much the same lines as those of David Lonsdale's later *Eyes
to See, Ears to Hear*. In view of the success of David's
book, the non-appearance of mine may not be too big a
loss; but I regret having missed the opportunity to acknowledge a group of people and an experiment which influenced
considerably my understanding of Ignatius.

The very mention, however, of the *Way* Community was
enough to stir the creative imagination of one of the recipients
of my Christmas letter, Billy Hewett,[2] who suggested that a
get-together of surviving members round a tape might
preserve memories otherwise in danger of being lost. Others,
Gerry Hughes, Jock Earle, Kathleen McGhee and Mary
Grant, found the idea appealing, as did I when I found that no
organization was to be asked of me ... The present notes
were intended as a preparation for this occasion.

---

2 [Billy Hewett, SJ, active in developing new methods of presenting Ignatian spirituality, particularly through music; he founded Inigo
Enterprises, partly for the publication of books and cassettes and partly
to organize courses and retreats.]

Background: although at that time I was James Walsh's
co-worker on *The Way* periodical, my memory of the pre-
history of the *Way* Community is a little uncertain, largely
because during a crucial four months I was out of the
country. The following may, therefore, be inaccurate on
points of detail and sequence; but I think, the essentials are
covered.

The *Way* Community arose from the situation of its
founder, Fr James Walsh, SJ, and from two concerns in
particular which were driving forces in his life. To most
Jesuits, James was primarily the editor of *The Way* periodical. The periodical was certainly mainly important for
James, but in its early years was a well administered enterprise demanding relatively little time of its editor; and, in
the years before the *Way* Community, James' main pre-
occupations were the organization of post-Vatican religious
renewal and the establishment of an 'Institute of Ignatian
spirituality' for the study and making of the *Exercises* and
to promote the study as a basis of religious renewal. When
I first knew him, James was an acknowledged expert in
constitutional revision; he was deeply involved in the
A.R.C. courses[3] in Rome, which were his model for a
series of shorter courses which he (we) ran in this country
with some acclaim. In contrast, the project of a centre had
not yet got off the ground.

After an abortive start at Heythrop,[4] the project entered
upon a slightly spectral form, existing mainly in James'
imagination, the 'Institute of Spiritual and Pastoral Special-
ization'. The situation changed decisively when James was
offered the use of Southwell House[5] and he assembled in
this situation a group with a view to staffing a resident insti-

---

3   [Apostolic Religious Communities: the first (longer) courses were orga-
    nized by the Sisters of Notre Dame in Rome in the seventies as a
    follow-up to the Council.]
4   [While the College was still based in Oxfordshire.]
5   [A house in Fitzjohn's Avenue, Hampstead, London, belonging to the
    Society of Jesus and used over the years for a great variety of purposes
    (retreats, student residence, and most recently for work with Youth,
    'The Hampstead Youth Project').]

tute of spirituality on those premise. The group would have himself as director, and on James' original plan Kathleen McGhee,[6] I think, was to serve as a retreat-giver; the administrator would be Mary Grant,[7] a fully trained psychologist; Jock Earle[8] he regarded as giving respectability to the group. This prospect was modified by a reversal of policy regarding the presence of scholastics in Southwell House. Although quarters were to be made available to the group, Southwell House could now only be the group's residence, not the centre of its apostolate.

Thus constituted, and on this understanding, the group held a series of meetings at Skelmorlie to take bearings and make some preliminary decisions. At the suggestion of Michael Reddy,[9] present as a friend and facilitator, the fateful decision was made to call ourselves 'The *Way* Community'. And I think it was at this time that it was decided that Kathleen McGhee and Gerry [W.] Hughes should go to Guelph [Canada], where Kathleen would make the *Exercises* and Gerry serve as a visiting director. Somewhere in the early stages of the group's history – shamefully, I forget when – Gerry and I were appointed Tertian Instructors,[10] a development which complicated and ultimately enriched the *Way* Community without altering its essential quality. How long the project might have survived if left to itself we were never allowed to discover, since it ran up against stiff opposition at the higher levels of Province authority and was disbanded. On the grounds for this opposition, more later.

6   [She has contributed to the *Memories*.]
7   [Mary Grant, a sister of the Sacred Heart; later working in Edinburgh.]
8   [George Earle, SJ [known as 'Jock'], 1925–2003, former Head Master at Stonyhurst and Provincial, a major figure in the recent history of the Jesuits in the UK.]
9   [Michael Reddy had been a member of the Society; on leaving he specialized in psychological counselling work, in particular using transactional analysis.]
10 [The appointment to St Beuno's came in 1976, but Michael had already had some experience as a Tertian Director: in Sunderland (1972–3) and in both Australia (1974) and Rhodesia (as it then was, 1975), but always with Jesuit Brothers, so usually three months at a time.]

The *Way* Community in retrospect: what were its main characteristics? And, what was the key to its particular challenge? At one level the *Way* Community was a group of apostolic religious who lived and worked together in quarters at Southwell House, forming a small experimental community which in many ways fitted a model being widely pioneered at that time in religious life. It was Eucharist-centred, self-servicing and self-catering, committed to an ideal of genuine friendship and a sharing of insights and experience in the context of a single conversational stream; it was also committed to an open house concept of hospitality. What was breaking new ground here was the fact of it being inter-congregational, men and women living and working together on a basis of total equality. Secondly, its purpose was to provide an environment ideally suited to studying, personally assimilating, experimenting with, and giving to others the *Spiritual Exercises* in an age when giving the *Exercises* were still a largely clerical and hence male-dominated ministry. To many people the idea of a nun retreat-giver was rather like a freakish para-liturgy. This idea poses questions and challenges for us even twenty years on in our own time. However, extravagant claims sometimes read into the very title, 'The *Way* Community', must be avoided. First we did not come together in order to experience mixed community for itself; nor were we setting up a model for all apostolic religious life. Indeed, the *Way* Community was not so much founded as allowed to happen. It was the obvious, and possibly only way, in which a particular apostolic group could attain its particular project in given circumstances. What happened, however, was in a modest and low-key way the appearance of a new kind of apostolic religious community: there were innumerable situations in which men and women religious both shared work and lived a family-like situation in the *Way* corridor of Southwell House. Thus we broke new ground. In doing so the *Way* Community would obviously affect people in many ways and what these may have been, in the form of new and unfamiliar challenges and disciplines and invitations to change, only individuals concerned will be able to testify.

For myself it must be added that in many respects, and two in particular, being 'mixed' made a particularly important, if not indispensable contribution to the capacity of the Community to be an agent of ministry and the dissemination of spirituality.

First, it was a community in which the very experience of community life was itself a formation in the spirituality of the *Exercises*. As someone put it, conversation in the *Way* Community, potentially at least, had something of the character of a running seminar on the *Exercises*. In a sense, the community was a distinctive culture shaped by the language of the *Exercises*. It was a community for which the *Exercises* were a culture.

One of the more important aspects of the developments in ministry taking place at this time was the inclusion of the activity of the non-clerical Christian. By the time of the *Way* Community much development in this field had already come about, regarding the ministry of the *Spiritual Exercises*. An undoubtedly significant factor was the development under John English of the Ignatian centre at Guelph, of which mention has already been made. The aim of this centre, I gather, was to involve in the ministry of the *Exercises* the people who previously had been allowed to receive them, mainly women. It would be extravagant, of course, to deny that such developments had already begun in this country already, but there is no doubt of the impetus it received from the *Way* Community, first through its own retreat-giving work and in facilitating groups. But in a sense, the Community's very existence was a challenge to some of the attitudes and agreed proprieties that held back the advance of an inclusive ministry.

How does the *Way* Community appear after an interval of twenty years or more? Does it still challenge us? Or have the challenges it raised lost relevance? In considering these questions, we must keep in mind shifts of opinion, in particular regarding residential communities, and the ideal of the radically mixed inter-congregational community.[11]

---

[11] [Unfortuntately Michael's account breaks off here. For an article celebrating the 25th birthday of *The Way*, cf. John Coventry, 'The Way, 1961–1986', *Letters and Notices* 87 (390), Easter 1986, pp. 117–28.]

§4 'My medical history'

Michael Ivens, SJ

1. Diary[12]

(i) An outline: 1990-2000

1990 Brain tumour discovered by Mr Chandra, ophthalmic consultant at St Asaph, during investigation of double vision. May 29. Operation at Walton Hospital for meningioma (later re-classified as 'cordoma'?) I am told that the tumour had formed round an artery, so that only partial removal was possible. After the operation I had a seizure and am technically epileptic, though I have never experienced further symptoms. The operation has left me without pituitary function and I was put by stages onto the following medication, which I understand I will remain on for life: Hydrocortisone – present dose 40mg; Thyroxine – present dose 150mcg; Epanutin – 200mgs; Sustenon (testosterone), per 21 days.

Since the operation I am regularly seen by the surgeon, Mr Shaw, and an endocrinologist, Dr McFarlane at Walton. Mr Chandra at St Asaph

---

[12] [Very typical of the man is the cool detachment with which he recorded the various stages of his medical history; among his Notes were (1) this short Diary, and also (2) the 'election' process with which he decided not to have a further operation.]

checks regularly for ophthalmic indications of the state of the tumour. I receive periodic brain scans. Though the tumour is mainly stable there have been indications of slight growth, which affect my eyesight (see below).

(ii) Summary of subsequent history

1990 Aug 29–31. Glan Clwyd. Treated for raised intra-cranial pressure.
Oct 11–18. Walton hospital. Tests for diabetes insipidus proved positive (eventually I recovered from this condition).

1993 Took part in growth hormone trial. At conclusion of the trial I elected, against advice of doctors, not to continue the treatment.

1995 December. Glan Clwyd hospital. Flu.

1996 November 5. Heart attack. Treated in Glan Clwyd. Beta blockers and aspirin prescribed. After a short time I was taken off the beta blockers. Later I was put onto – and remain on – anti-cholesterol medication by Dr MacFarlane.

1997 April. Operation for cataract. Right eye.
August, November. Twice admitted to Glan Clwyd with severe gastric symptoms and rigors. Kidneys suspected. Tests made but diagnosis never clarified.
November As result of scan Mr Shaw confirmed that the tumour was putting pressure on optic nerves and that should my eyesight continue to deteriorate the question of saving it by further intra-cranial surgery might arise. He stressed the high risk of such an operation.

1998 January. Since eyesight was not continuing to deteriorate, Mr Shaw decided that there was no need for further surgery.
February. Consultation with specialist re. abdominal hernia, Consultation arranged with anaesthetist who declined to accept me except in an emergency.

April. Registered partially sighted.
September. Cataract operation on left eye.
November. Question of growth hormone raised again. Dr MacFarlane anxious that I should go onto it, and that my case should be used to persuade Welsh authority to fund growth hormone. I now inject myself with growth hormones last thing each night.

1999 April. A heavy fall on the front steps of St Beuno's resulting in two minor facial fractures but also eventual loss of vision in left eye.
My present situation is fairly stable. My energy levels are very low but sufficient for my work, provided I am not pressured by deadlines etc. I have no sight in the left eye but workable tunnel vision in the right. Prognosis regarding right eye seems impossible to make. I am told that I could still have effective sight for years or completely lose sight with little warning.
Present medication: Aspirin 150mg.; Hydrocortisone 40mg.; Thyroxine 150mcg.; Epanutin 200mg.; Lescol 40 mg.; Growth Hormone: daily injection; Sustenon, injection per 21 days.

2001 March 15. Routine check-up at H. M. Stanley reveals marked reduction of visual field together with other evidence of sight deterioration.
May 23. Appointment with Mr Shaw, who had received a letter from St Asaph about the above tests and ordered an 'MRI' scan.
June 27. MRI scan Glan Clwyd.
July 25. Neuro-endocrinology clinic. Mr Shaw confirmed that the tumour had grown significantly, raising the question again of surgery to save my eyesight (see November 1997). He stressed again the dangers, mentioning specifically stroke and impairment to speech. I was asked to 'think' about the matter.
Another question raised at this session was the

marked fatigue I have been experiencing over the past months and whether this is connected with recent reductions in my thyroxine dosage. Dr McFarlane inclined to think the cause might be in the heart. I was put onto 'Frusemine' (one tablet daily) with instructions to refer to GP and possibly the Glan Clwyd heart consultant.

August 22. Visit to Walton Centre. Reflecting on the situation as presented above, I decided to let nature take its course with my sight rather than incur the risks of surgery. The consultant (a stand-in for Mr Shaw but seemingly well briefed on my case) told me that precisely by not having surgery I could bring on the very conditions I was hoping to avoid by not having it. I said I would like more time to think and he arranged for a second brain scan. Much, I gather, will depend on whether the tumour is still growing. A few days previously Dr Salusbury had taken me off growth hormone on the grounds that its use is counter-indicated in the case of a growing brain tumour. Dr McFarlane admitted the possibility of growth hormone affecting a tumour.
(I am left feeling that I have done my bit for growth hormone.)

2. Surgery: yes/no? [an exercise in discernment]

Saturday, 28 July

Three levels of question:
data (mainly medical); attitude (indifference especially); God's will

1. Medical prognosis. Two things seem clear:
   (i) I should assume that without surgery I shall go blind eventually, but it does not seem possible to estimate how soon.

(ii) An operation to save my sight would involve certain dangers: that the operation might itself result in blindness, that it could result in a stroke or in damage to the speech centre. Danger to life does not, however, seem to be 'beyond the ordinary'. The dangers to be taken into account seem to be mainly the above-named.

2. My own attitudes
On being first faced with this situation, my reaction was to opt against the operation and to let nature take its course. This seemed reasonable on the grounds that in relation to possible consequences of the operation (including instant blindness caused by the operation itself) to leave my eyesight to nature, with a near certainty of gradual blindness, seems the lesser evil. I realize however that there was a strong element of instinct in this and in particular that I was not approaching the questions from a standpoint of indifference. Various things at the moment are standing in the way of indifference: Blindness is a considerably less unattractive option than the possible alternatives. I think I can offer myself to God for a life without sight. I don't feel able to do the same with regard to the other disabilities. Why? Do I consider blindness preferable to physical indignity?

Am I free in my attitudes from an element of attention-seeking and self-dramatization?

Later in the day, I pondered the case for taking the risk of stroke etc. Conversation with Mary brought home the realities involved and put me back to the option for blindness.

Sunday 29 July

Evening and night.
The real implications of blindness came home to me with a sudden shock. I did offer my sight. A very mixed experience – feelings of oppression and enormous sadness, tears

yet consolation within it all, and a peaceful sense that this might be God's will. 'Yours was the gift; to you I give it back. Give me only your love and your grace...'

At any rate I am now in a different 'place' regarding blindness. There is nothing facile now about the way I am feeling about it. I don't *think* I am in denial any longer.

I still can't offer myself for the alternative. Does this mean that I am not required to or that I don't want to?

A thought on the 'third time' side. Two relevant questions are: what would enable me to be more useful? what would give a better personal life quality? As I perceive blindness now, it is by no means clear that from the quality of life viewpoint, to be smitten by stroke and impaired speech, while being still being able to see, would be worse than blindness. On the other hand if I go blind but remain otherwise unimpaired I could – and would – pick up the one-to-one kinds of ministry that are certainly of service to others.

29 June–11 August

Various thoughts and feelings keep coming and going.

With regard to blindness, in spite of the acceptance mentioned above, for much of the time I simply find it hard to believe it will happen. Eyesight may be deteriorating gradually, maybe the situation is stable – various DIY tests are inconclusive. If the tumour has stabilized, might there not be years of such sight as I have, before further pressure on the optic nerves destroys my sight for good ...

I suspect that elements of self-interest come into my ability to accept the prospect of blindness, which colludes, possibly, with escapist tendencies.

I have sometimes come nearer to being able to accept the possible effects of the operation – stroke or speech impairment. Yet I can't quite make the breakthrough, or if I seem to for a moment can't sustain it. Offering my power of speech it was as though the answer was 'Thank you, but I want you to keep that; but as for sight, well perhaps that's a different matter...' Is all this just fantasy? Most difficult of all. Should I make the operation an act of trust in God? What will happen will be what he wants to happen. Tempting Providence – or trusting? Is this, as it were, unloading responsibility? Do I remain responsible for the consequences of my own actions? Again am I really capable of this kind of trust or am I play-acting?

What I keep coming back to, and what seems most to give peace, is the position I tell other people I have reached – and everyone seems to think right, viz to opt not to risk my other faculties even at the price of certain loss of sight. The reason – that I can be more useful with wits and no sight than with sight and no wits – even if a bit dramatically put, does seem the direction 'indicated by reason'. Moreover the criterion is that of service, not personal quality of life – which seems right.

August 18

I realize what a horribly serious decision I am having to make.

There are things in me that make the prospects of blindness tolerable. Thinking of the beginnings, it will be a kind of adventure – learning new skills etc. The reality however is total night, unmitigated darkness for life. The light will go out and I shall see nothing more until I see God. Can I live with equanimity in this night for ten ... twenty years with never sight of a page of print? never able to write the things I would like to write – maybe never able to master the new tricks sufficiently to write anything? Will I sometimes be frightened? Will I improve as a person – or deteriorate into frustration, morbidity, ungraciousness, etc.?

I need the assurance that, as far as I can possibly know, it is what God wants.

From time to time another thought steals in on me. While

'no' to surgery is an option for near-certain blindness, the chances are that surgery would be successful. (If the odds were not in favour of success Mr Shaw would have made his own decision not to operate.) Yet. I sometimes behave as though I were choosing between two certitudes instead of between a certitude and an odds-against possibility. So is there something mean-spirited about refusal? The question agitates me.

On the other hand is there something ultimately false about the peace I feel most of the time with the blindness option. (Do I actually believe it is going to happen?)

Sunday 19 [August]

Able – I think – to be quiet and listen. 'Speak Lord!' What seemed to come through was that it was not God's will that I commit the health service to huge expense, occupy a hospital bed possibly for weeks, put the Beuno's community under great stress and Mary in an impossible situation for months at least – all in a sense to challenge God to bring me safely through a dangerous gamble ... To let nature run its course is the humbler way.

> I also began to see what a viable 'rule of life' for a blind person might be.
> All this left me feeling peaceful.

Later in the morning had a conversation with John Lynch who became animated when I mentioned the speech risk and advised me strongly to hang onto my speech, whatever the price.

21st August

Made my 'offering', not with absolute confidence of having been free, attentive and docile, but at least with a sense of having tried.

All the time attitudes have oscillated between thinking of the decision I have made as being so obvious that discernment is hardly called for, and at the other pole, seeing the issue as carrying a responsibility which for all my efforts, I have not taken fully seriously. Anyway I have taken a decision which will result almost certainly in my some time going blind. I have now to commit myself – but peacefully, realistically and without frenzy – to the tasks of the 'remains of the day' , be those remains brief or extended.

§5 Homily at Requiem of Michael Ivens

Gerard W. Hughes, SJ,
St Beuno's, 17 September 2005

A welcome to you all to this celebration of Michael's living and dying in Christ.

When I began to prepare this homily, I stared at a blank piece of paper, then I spoke with Michael, 'What do you want me to say about you at your Requiem?' The answer was instant, 'As little as possible!' 'At least, give me some general headings.' 'I would like you to thank all the people I have met in life, to thank God for giving us Godself in all things, and I would like the day of my burial to be a day of celebration.'

There is not time to thank everyone by name, but we thank Michael's brother, Peter, who is with us today, their parents and all those who cared for him, nurtured and taught him. Michael was most grateful for many things in Jesuit life, most especially in the last sixteen years when his health began to deteriorate. He loved St Beuno's where he had lived since 1976 and was most grateful for the care and kindness he received from the whole community here, which now includes among the retreat-giving staff many who are not Jesuit. As important, if not more important than the retreat-givers, are all the kitchen staff, all who administer, clean and maintain the building and make the house such a welcoming place. Throughout his illness Michael was most appreciative of the medical care he received through the Denbigh practice, local hospitals, the nursing care, and he appreciated and delighted especially in the gift of Lennie, his guide dog for the blind, officially registered as 'Lennie Ivens'. I know that his greatest thanks go to Sr Mary Reidy, who nursed him devotedly for sixteen years, all day and sometimes much of the night. I also know that both Mary and Michael are most grateful to Fr James Chaning-Pearce for all the support he has given them, especially in the last three years of Michael's total blindness.

On his father's side, Michael was born of a Portuguese family of army generals and explorers. Michael inherited the explorer spirit, but the military genes passed him by! His mother was from Bolton, in Lancashire, her family from a long line of Anglican vicars. She was born in Russia, where her father was working as an engineer. He ran into trouble with the English consul because he supported the Russian workers in their complaints. Peter tells me that Michael, before he was a teenager, was writing poetry, playing Mozart, painting, and that he wrote a version of the Ten Commandments, adding his own eleventh – 'Thou shalt always be kind to animals.' As a youngster, he was fascinated with astronomy and with sailing. Besides other pet animals he had a rat which slept in his bed and ate from the same plate at meal times! On one occasion his mother had prepared a tea party for friends. Michael inspected the set table, removed the teapot from under the cosy, put the rat in its place, then escaped, but within earshot of the screams of the assembled guests. The cub mistress expelled him from the cubs, because of his continual unpunctuality, a punishment which did not deter him in the slightest in later life. His Jesuit headmaster wrote two letters to his parents threatening expulsion. One cause was his disruption of classes by making animal noises. The headmaster was later asked why he had such a down on Michael and answered, 'Because there is a very dangerous streak of independence in him.' How right the headmaster was about the independence and how wrong about its nature!

Born in 1933, Michael entered the Jesuit noviceship in

1951 with many others. After philosophy at Heythrop, he read history at Oxford, then taught for two years at Stonyhurst before theology at Fourvière, Lyons, where he was ordained in 1966. It was at Stonyhurst, where I was also teaching, I first came to know and appreciate him. Three incidents give something of his character: the first was of meeting him one morning just after 6.30 a.m. He had the appearance of an unmade bed, his hair dishevelled, hair and clothing spattered with paint. He had spent the night painting stage scenery. Sleep was never a priority with Michael. The second event was a visit to his room, which was full of boys, a rat, a snake, and a tamed bird. He was especially popular with boys who found regimentation of any kind difficult. The third incident was a conversation. He had been away for two nights searching for a summer campsite for the scouts. 'Where did you stay on the two nights?' I asked. 'In a telephone kiosk,' he replied, reckoning this to be a perfectly sensible thing to do. Personal comfort was never a priority with Michael. He seemed quite unaware of his gifts. Years later, he remarked, 'It is a pity that we no longer have eccentric Jesuits around!'

After tertianship in 1968, he spent a year as chaplain at Manchester University, was later Spiritual Father at Campion Hall and began working with Fr James Walsh as co-editor of *The Way*, the spirituality periodical that James Walsh had founded. He also ran a tertianship, a final year of training for Jesuit brothers, first in England, then in Australia, and a third in what was then Rhodesia. In 1975, he joined the *Way* Community,[13] an experimental community founded by Fr James Walsh, for the study and promotion of the *Spiritual Exercises*. The Community included Srs Mary Grant (Sacred Heart) and Kathleen McGhee (Sister of Notre Dame), together with Frs Jock Earle, Billy Hewett, Michael Ivens, Felix McGowan and myself. At the end of this Mass, Sr Kathleen McGhee will

---

[13] [See §3.]

speak on Michael's role in the *Way* Community.[14] All of us enjoyed the years we had together in the *Way* Community where we learned much from our conversations with one another, reflecting on our own experience of making and giving the Exercises. We also laughed a lot. These were very happy years for Michael. In 1976, while still remaining members of the *Way* Community, Michael and I were appointed to run the Jesuit tertianship at St Beuno's, a nine-month spirituality course, which we were encouraged to adapt from the monastic model, which it had become, to a training more in line with the 34th Jesuit Congregation, which had taken place in 1974.

In setting up a modern tertianship Michael and I encountered many difficulties from the house, which did not take kindly to change, being a retirement house for ageing Jesuits. On the first morning of the first Tertianship one older Father, walking through the refectory, declared loudly and angrily, 'Can't move for bloody foreigners!' There were the intercultural difficulties of an international tertianship, as well as the aftermath of the Second Vatican Council in the Church. In all this, Michael began to show those qualities which became more pronounced in later years. He was 'a contemplative in action',[15] by which I do not mean he was having beautiful contemplative experiences while floating above the mess of life, but that his whole attitude to everything tended to be contemplative. He did not approach life and its problems with a set agenda: he approached with a sense of wonder, he let the facts impinge on him rather than he arranging the facts to suit his own preconceived ideas. He had a wonderfully open mind and heart. His humour flowed from this disposition: he could view reality around him and himself from a standpoint which was outside himself, hence his ability to see the absurd nature of so much that engrosses our ego-bound minds.

[14] [§6 Memories.]
[15] [This phrase to describe a typical Jesuit, *contemplativus in actione*, is attributed to Jerome Nadal, an early Jesuit very close to St Ignatius.]

In 1978, after two years with tertians, I was invited to turn St Beuno's into a Jesuit spirituality centre. Michael continued to run the tertianship on his own and Fr Patrick Purnell came to join us, but he was also appointed Minister of the house, a full-time job in itself. As to turning St Beuno's into a spirituality centre, all that we could do, without a staff and without money, was to dream about what might be. We were always joined in our deliberations by Beuno, a very beautiful, intelligent, but badly trained Labrador dog whom, on occasion, we dressed in a Roman collar that contrasted well with his jet black coat, with spectacles on his nose, to remind us that we were engaged in serious business. Michael loved conversation. He would never dismiss any suggestion, however outrageous it might, at first, seem to be. This gift made him such an outstandingly good spiritual director and retreat-giver, for he enabled others to discover for themselves the nature of what they were experiencing. He never preached at, nor coerced in any way. His manner was always gentle, never intrusive, yet he had the ability to ask the key questions that brought enlightenment to the other. He could lead people to freedom because he himself was free, free to give his whole attention.

The secret of his gift as retreat-giver and spiritual director lay in his inner disposition, his living of the first beatitude, 'How happy are you who are poor: yours is the kingdom of God,' which means 'How happy are those who really do know their own fragility for they come to know that God truly is their rock, their refuge, their strength.' He was outstandingly generous in the time and attention he gave to others. He knew exhaustion, but found it difficult to relax. On one occasion, after an exhausting day, he said to me, 'I think I've lost my zeal for souls'.

Michael's book *Understanding the Spiritual Exercises* is the result of years of study of the text, but much more from his years of giving the Spiritual Exercises to a wide variety of people of all Christian denominations and none, and from reflection and conversation on that experience. There was an extraordinary contrast in Michael's life: his perfectionism over the written word and about the tidiness of our thinking; his carelessness about his own living style, dressing style, his sleeping and eating, the chaos of his room and disorder of his work files. This contrast disappeared when Michael had a brain tumour operation in 1990 and Sr Mary Reidy appeared.

For years before his brain tumour operation, Michael was afflicted by occasional and very severe migraines. He could speak about his illness without ever showing any sign whatever of self-sympathy. In pain, he was still able to speak of it as though from outside himself, as though discussing a case which he found interesting. He phoned me one night after the consultant had described the nature of the tumour operation he was about to undergo and the possible after effects. The prognosis was terrifying. Michael spent the night in the St Beuno's chapel. After the operation he had lost the sight of one eye and the other was damaged, and had lost his pituitary gland, leaving him dependent on medication for the rest of his life. It was in these years following the operation that he wrote and completed his *Understanding the Spiritual Exercises*, an achievement that had eluded him in his years of health. In the years of the *Way* Community many of us had offered to take over his manuscript, edit it, then present it to him for approval. We failed. It was Fr Joe Munitiz who, years later, succeeded in wresting the manuscript from Michael and, with he help of Fr Billy Hewett, having it published by Gracewing.

For the last three years Michael suffered terribly. He became totally blind while reading a book, his hearing was impaired, his mobility gradually diminished, his memory, formerly so good, began to fail, yet even till the day of his death he would have periods of lucidity when he seemed fully aware of his state. In recent months I used to come away from Michael with the opening lines of the *Dream of Gerontius*[16] in my head:

---

[16] [The poem of John Henry Newman, later set to music by Edward Elgar.]

Jesu, Maria, I am near to death,
And thou art calling me; I know it now.
Not by the token of this faltering breath,
This chill at heart, this dampness on my brow ...
'Tis this new feeling, never felt before ...
This strange and uttermost collapse of all that makes me man.

I never heard Michael whinge, although I did hear him say
clearly, 'I am falling apart.' I hated seeing him like this
but, strangely, never felt depressed. Towards the end, he
would occasionally show signs of tetchiness and complain
to Mary, or even at Mary. Mary was always wonderful and
reminded me of God, as God is described in the King
James' version of the Book of Wisdom (11:24) 'God
winketh at our transgressions that we may amend.' Mary
would let Michael complain, as pleased as though he were
hurling compliments, then say 'Now Michael, I would like
you to do this' and Michael would comply without a word!

It has been a privilege for me to give this homily, to have
had so many years working closely with him. It has been a
privilege for St Beuno's to have him here for twenty-nine
years. Michael is now no longer restricted. He will
continue to bless this house, its work and all who come to
it.

I thank God for his gifts, his idiosyncracies, his childlike
simplicity, his charm, his insight and wisdom. We are glad
for him now that every tear is wiped away and that he can
now see You, our God, as you are, and can know his at-
one-ness with You in whom all creation has its being.

As I finish, I can hear Michael's words and intonation as
he says, what he always said on our parting, 'Goodbye,
Gerry, Be in touch.' Michael, you will always be in touch
with us. Help us always to keep in touch with you.

§6 Memories

David Barchard [former pupil]

We always say people whom we have lost are unique and, indeed, all of us are, but Michael was truly unique in a particular way. He has a place in my memories which is quite different from anyone else's and is really impossible to categorize, but I am so grateful that for at least a year or two of my life I knew him well. He left in me enduring memories which are quietly but emphatically inspirational.

He was not my teacher. I rather think we met in the Scouts, another temporary phase in my life, but I got to know him best through his coterie or painting circle, which in retrospect looks somewhat like a remedial group or even a mission. I have never, before or since, had much to do with painting, so it was a very vivid time for me and I recall with lasting astonishment his final remarks to me when he left Stonyhurst, that I should continue with painting because, contrary to his initial judgement, I had some talent for it. I think this was a compliment in excess of what I deserved, but I really appreciated it.

As a friend and mentor, he offered constant humour, wisdom, and commitment to his faith, which was shrewd, practical, realistic, and very human. I even think that by encouraging me to look at art history and books, he may have played an indirect part in steering me to a lifelong

interest in Turkey – which sprang from looking at a book
of Byzantine history that year.

He managed to be completely unassuming and yet as
solid as a rock in his views on things. He introduced us to
L. S. Lowry, when Lowry was completely unknown: 'I
think he deserves to be recognized.' And despite his sense
of humour and irony, I never detected a single note of jeal-
ousy or envy towards anyone else: now that really is
unique!

I never forgot our conversations, and remained a little in
contact with him over the years, though I think we met only
once, if at all, after Stonyhurst. I was grieved to learn from
friends of his afflictions over the last few years, and always
meant to do more to renew contact with him. Happily I did
get round to writing a letter late last year and got (what I
did not expect) a reply directly from him in the form of a
very nice e-mail.

It is strange to feel so much loss for someone that one
has not seen for about four decades. I have prayed for him
and remembered him in my prayers. I know he will have
remembered us in his. I am very grateful that I knew him.

Mark Hackett, SJ

I used to be in the room next to Michael Ivens on the inner
circle[17] at Heythrop and we became good friends. At the
end of one Barmouth *villa*[18] we still had some money left
over and we decided to use it for a day's sailing on the river

[17] [The phrase 'inner circle' is simply an architectural reference; a number
of the rooms occupied by the students looked onto an inner quadrangle
of what would once have been the service quarters of Heythrop Manor
(then the home of Heythrop College); the College moved to London in
1970, but kept its name.]
[18] [For many years it was the custom for Jesuit students to be sent for a
fortnight's holiday at the Province holiday house in Barmouth (N.
Wales): the term for this was the annual *villa*.]
[19] [At the time Rector of the Jesuit house of studies.]

in Oxford. It was at the time when [Fr] Jack Diamond[19] had been trying to discourage hitchhiking into Oxford from Broadstone Hill. Joe Laishley and I were hiding in the hedge while Michael was trying to hitch. A car pulled up. It was the Rector. 'Are you going into Oxford?' asked Michael. 'No, but I'm going back to the college,' said Jack. 'That's no good. I'm going to Oxford,' said Michael and shut the door. Jack drove off. We had a nice day's sailing.

Michael disliked any form of hypocrisy. One should be genuine. A spade should be exactly that. He once told me that one should never give *ferulas*[20] to someone unless one had been at the receiving end oneself. Then one knew exactly what one was doing.

An Australian sister who had made the Long Retreat [of thirty days] with him told me this story. About half way into the retreat she was getting somewhat strained. Michael suggested that she should take a few days off. Did she know anyone she could spend a few days with. 'I have a friend in Paris,' she volunteered. 'Ideal!' said Michael. Has anyone else had a director make a similar recommendation?

Michael was no disciplinarian and I gathered his teaching practice in a somewhat unruly East End school was a bit harrying. Hearing that the examiners were to come the next day to make their assessment of him, Michael pleaded with them to behave themselves the next day. One of the worst boys in the back row put up his hand. 'You don't need to worry, sir. We won't let you down.'

David Harold-Barry, SJ [now Zimbabwe Province]

I have visited St Beuno's a number of times in the last ten years or so, and always was given a little time with Michael. On the first occasion we were aroused in the

---

20 [The *ferula* was a strap used to chastise misdemeanours in Jesuit colleges; blows were delivered on the culprit's outstretched hand, and they were also called *ferulas*.]

middle of the night for fire drill, and I found that I and one or two other visitors were among the few who did everything we were supposed to do, like gathering outside in a brisk Welsh morning around 2.00 a.m. Since nothing seemed to be happening we returned to our beds, but not before I met Michael in one of those huge Beuno's passages. 'There isn't a fire,' he said, 'there never is. When there is one it (the system) doesn't pick it up. I know because I once set my waste paper basket alight . . . It is like hell. It could happen, but you know it won't.'

Years later when he was blind he still spoke with a joy that showed up how he savoured life even in little incidents. He did not just tell a story, but every sentence was relished. One such occasion was when he was with Joe Laishley,[21] in the Aegean and the engine in the boat failed. His description of Joe calling out to a passing fisherman in Koine Greek for help just made one weak with laughter.

To say he was always cheerful doesn't express that amazing calm and deep trust that he showed all the time. His suffering in his latter years seemed to increase his wonderful presence of joy and trust. He talked and wrote about the *Exercises*, but more than that he lived them so totally.

Billy Hewett, SJ [friend, colleague and editor-publisher]

My earliest memory of Michael is of my being appointed as a novice to reduce his ultra-pseudo upper-class pronunciation to that of standard BBC (rather in the style of Laurence Olivier) in which I had been well trained. Michael in later life amused his many admirers with an expert imitation of my rather clipped Public School pronunciation! Where Michael acquired his pronunciation, God

---

[21] [Fr Francis Laishley, SJ (always known as 'Joe'), a contemporary and friend, later professor of theology at Heythrop College in London.]

knows (Upminster?). But it was very pronounced and individual, and the Jesuit 'English' Province, as it was then, was very keen that all its members should speak standard BBC (then King's) English of which I was a perfect, expensively educated, exemplar. Another candidate was a broadly accented Glaswegian Scotsman, old enough to be my father, who totally resisted my expert tuition, and Michael equally resisted my efforts, and retained his utterly unique intonation until his dying day. It was often imitated, but remained utterly inimitable. And I am glad I failed because it was so much a living part of Michael: in Paulo Freire's terms, he had found his voice from an early age and spoke consistently with it until his dying day. For Michael was a man as remarkable for his consistency as he was for his integrity.

My next spontaneous memory of Michael is of him as a *sailor*; though not a natural athlete or team games player, he had a wiry strength that made him an extraordinarily reliable skipper of many dodgy sailing boats, as well as of some highly streamlined yachts. I experienced his totally reliable mastery of both, from holidays at Brixham [Barmouth?] to an unlikely and exotic holiday in which he, Joe Laishley and I took on and beat three admirals in a competition in the Aegean. Michael was that wonderful combination of absolutely outstanding first-class competence with utterly shabby, desperately unpresentable squalor.

This was particularly apparent when, as fellow scholastics in the 1950s at Stonyhurst, we were, as happened to scholastics in those days, loaded with all the jobs that nobody else was willing – or even remotely competent – to undertake. In this case, Michael was told to look after the scouts. The scouts then were a very poor relation to the domineering Combined Cadet Force with its long tradition of VCs. For many of the more perceptive, if less orderly, youths of the time, scouting was a wonderfully adventurous and undisciplined way of escape. Michael's room at the top of the West Wing was a haven of delight, not least among its inhabitants, apart from Michael, was an affectionate white rat which scurried around amidst the squalor of the room. In those days there were open fires on which bread was toasted and spread with anything anyone could provide. Nescafé had just come in, a much appreciated delicacy and an alternative to the watery variety provided by the school authorities. One twelve-year-old remembers with delight the sight of Michael peeling from his coal-scuttle a congealed spoonful of the rare delicacy. I remember too the courageous, if foolhardy abandon, with which Michael was the first to test the ancient fire escape harness from the dormitory windows (six-storeys high), a courageous example which the boys eagerly, and even I (less eagerly, and shaking with well-founded fear) then followed.

In the short-lived and experimental *Way* Community, Michael and I were the youngest male members, younger brothers one might say, of this close-knit (family) experiment in applying the highly individualistic *Spiritual Exercises* of St Ignatius to practical community living. For the participants it was a wonderfully enriching spiritual experience but too far ahead of its times to be positively accepted by the Province as a whole.

I was a regular visitor to Michael in his long years of physical decline and ever-increasing spiritual maturity under the devoted care of Mary Reidy at St Beuno's. With her very positive help and the tenacious expertise of Joe Munitiz I am not unwilling to claim responsibility, as Michael acknowledges in his Introduction, for the eventual production of Michael's supreme work and monument, *Understanding the Spiritual Exercises*. I am ashamed to say that at times, in impatient desperation, at the umpteenth re-writing of most of the chapters, I bullied him by saying such things as, 'If you can't come to the next editorial meeting with a final version don't come at all.' I know this hurt Michael much more than I intended but in the end, with other more subtle and less violent means, we did, between us, produce one of the finest commentaries on the *Exercises*, sufficiently contemporary as well as sufficiently scholarly to be of universal value for at least another decade or two. Michael possessed that rare combination of careful Ignatian scholarship and hands-on varied experience in actually giving the *Exercises* to participants throughout the world: to the great variety of people who came to St Beuno's as well as to the tertians of Australia, South Africa, Ireland, England. This was partly thanks to the great reputation inherited from Paul Kennedy, whom Michael much admired and indeed in some obvious ways resembled.

Apart from all this I remember Michael as an extraordinarily encouraging – as well as challenging – Spiritual Director. Not that he would have put great emphasis on the title 'director', or even on that of 'spiritual', at least in its more rarefied use, but much more on being a very human and honest 'friend in the Lord'. My personal debt to him is beyond reckoning and if I have achieved anything of value in my life it is for the part I played in the publishing of *Understanding the Spiritual Exercises*.

Kathleen McGhee, Sister of Notre Dame [co-worker; she spoke the following words at the funeral]

There will be as many stories floating around about Michael Ivens as there are people in this chapel this morning – and more. They will be told and re-told, invented and grow; the same story will be told differently by each one of us, and each of us will know that our version is the authentic one.

Michael with all his eccentricities and, well, unique way of being, provided the very quintessential stuff of story to the anecdote maker. But he himself was not an anecdote trader: 'I am not an anecdote man myself,' he would say. For this reason, I am not going to go that route, but rather to venture a little onto his preferred route, which was always about the meaning of things: 'What is the essence?' and 'Why?'

Maybe there are several answers but to me two are of great importance and were, I know, also to Michael: our shared experience of the *Way* Community,[22] and our friendship, which survived thirty-one years of knowing, of working, and, in our own way, of loving one another. The *Way* Community was very important for all eight of us who were part of it. It was certainly extremely important for Michael, and interestingly, it became increasingly significant for him with his long reflection in these later years. And it changed my life. I ask myself, 'What did we do?' Well, we worked, or course, gave the *Exercises*, retreats, courses, etc.; we made an attempt at living in community, but above all we talked a lot. We all talked a lot but when others flagged, Michael and I with a little more youth on our sides (and with Michael having no sense of time of day) often talked well into the night. What about? Well, about all kinds of things, but most of all about the *Exercises*. I had just discovered them and his intellectual thirst for them, together with my new found enthusiasm, kept us going for hours ... and years actually. What did they mean? And what excitement at every new insight! Michael always, wanting the truth of it.

He had such a thirst for Truth! That is why anecdotes were not his currency; he wanted the truth of it in ideas and relationships. It was why people found him such a good listener – he listened for their truth; and that's what made him such a compassionate companion to such a variety of people. It was also why it took him so long to complete any piece of writing (to the frustration of many editors and publishers). He wanted to get it right and wanted to be sure it was still right in ten or twenty years. I used to say to him, 'Michael, you could write another article in ten or twenty years with your developed thought.' But no, he thought that just too slovenly!

And of course, because he was human he did not always get it right. I have rarely known anyone who, when he knew he was wrong, especially in relationships, just had to

---

[22] [For more information on this, see §3.]

remedy it. And that made him very forgiving and very loving. In thirty-one years of friendship we made our mistakes and forgave them, though he was much better at that than I . . . it was the staff of our life. He was full of life and he gave me a lot of life. I know many put him on a pedestal . . . the pedestal of knowledge and insight; and he certainly earned that right with his lifetime's contribution to the *Exercises* and the understanding of Ignatius. But for me he was never on a pedestal. He stood beside me, a friend full of humour, eccentricity, vulnerability. He was different, but very warm and loving.

That is how I knew him and know him still; that was our way, our truth and our life, throughout the years. As he lay peacefully dying and I was saying my own goodbye, I found myself saying, as he always did, 'We'll be in touch.' I think we always will be. And I hope each one of you will be, too. Michael never forgot anyone he had met. He will remember us all.

Gero McLoughlin, SJ [colleague]

In writing of early Jesuit history, Fr Polanco noted that Ignatius 'always remained calm in mind and countenance'. I cannot judge whether this description applied equally to Michael Ivens, given that I would not count myself as having been among his close friends. However, proposed as a contemporary ideal, I remember Michael as the Jesuit who, in my experience, most nearly embodied that Ignatian characteristic.

I had met Michael as early as the 1960s at Campion Hall, Oxford, but I came to know him much better twenty years later when on the staff at St Beuno's from 1984 to 1991. After that, I did not see him much until I visited him regularly in the last few summers of his life.

In my own mind, I associate Michael's serenity with my impression that he was the least judgemental person I have ever known. He was so, in part, because he never made the mistake of confusing *holiness* with psychological and emotional *wholeness*. He did not, of course, underrate the importance of such integration, stressing, for example, the necessity of psychological balance for certain ways of life such as that of enclosed contemplatives. He realized that there is a psychological explanation for the sort of people we are, but for him it was not the final one. For Michael, life was a gradually unfolding mystery, revealing itself not despite human frailties and weaknesses, but because there is a more significant narrative for human experience than psychological interpretation: the narrative of grace redeeming human limitations. Of this, his long experience in helping others by means of the *Spiritual Exercises* assured him.

Thus, when a Jesuit colleague (now dead) was appointed to a senior post and some difficulties arose, Michael, instead of joining in negative and personally directed comment, remarked simply that he felt the man was 'emotionally too complex for the responsibilities entrusted to him'. He seemed not to doubt that in other circumstances, perhaps equally difficult, that person would manifest qualities no psychological expertise could explain. Ultimately (and unsurprisingly in my view) Michael's view was vindicated. The circumstances of that Jesuit's later life became complicated and painful. However, those changed circumstances evoked from him a humility that verged on the saintly, a humility completely unsuspected by earlier critics.

Michael's insight into the difference between the truth about a person's life and the more apparent circumstances in which their lives are caught up was, I feel, the principal motive for his devoting so much time and effort to those psychologically or emotionally burdened (to a greater or lesser degree). He was never derogatory of them. He never indulged in dismissive epithets such as sometimes can be employed to provide a release from the labour both of comprehending another person's experience and of being compassionate towards them.

No doubt partly an innate personal trait (manifested in

unfailing courtesy), Michael's attitude to others was corroborated by years of giving the *Spiritual Exercises*. I think it is not too strong to say that Michael loved the *Spiritual Exercises*. He profoundly respected their unique qualities, their potential for transforming a person's perception of God's relationship, and thus of the way in which they could foster a greater freedom to engage with the real world. He passed on his respect for the *Spiritual Exercises* to those fortunate enough to be supervised by him in giving them. He conveyed very clearly his belief that the *Spiritual Exercises* had a distinctive dynamic. He thought a giver of the Exercises was responsible for helping someone to experience that dynamic. He was bemused when he heard of people giving the *Spiritual Exercises* who had, in his view, 'short-changed' the person they were supposedly helping. This he felt when he heard of someone who considered that such was the impact of the Third Week, for the person being guided, that such a person should be allowed to continue in and 'complete' the Exercises without going on to the Fourth Week and the *Contemplatio*. Of that particular case, Michael remarked simply that it represented 'abandonment of responsibility'.

Those claiming to find in latter-day wisdoms a quality of insight merely hinted at in the *Spiritual Exercises* equally bemused him. Kathleen McGhee recalled at Michael's funeral that he was not a man given to anecdote; still less was he given to nostalgia. However, his speculation on known facts as, for example, the attempt to relate such latter-day wisdoms to giving the *Spiritual Exercises* verged on the surreal and was highly diverting. He entertained, equally, even in his latter years, when describing dilemmas that faced him. His account of trying to maintain concord by ensuring that two of his friends never discovered what the other believed about the Church became something of a saga.

After 1991, as I have said, I saw Michael at regular but widely spaced intervals. His progressive decline was unmistakeable. However it seemed to me that his belief in the blessing of what was, to outward appearances, a severely diminished and battered life barely changed. In this he was a powerful witness to the Ignatian conviction of accepting sickness 'as a gift from the hand of our Creator and Lord, since it is a gift no less than is health'. It was as though he viewed himself from the perspective he had previously used in helping others.

In writing of patience, the contemporary Italian author Enzo Bianchi has suggested that patience includes the 'art of taking a step back', in order to see the entire picture, and of accepting the incompleteness of the present; and that in this humility we confess that the divine plan of salvation has not yet been fully accomplished. This was the mind I feel Michael brought to his entire ministry, a mind in which I hope, at the end, he found his own peace.

Joseph A. Munitiz, SJ

Although Michael had been a fellow-novice with me, 1951–2, and we advanced step-by-step in the training until the end of regency, 1962, we were never very close. During those years I admired him as a brilliant speaker and actor, very gifted intellectually and socially (particularly with the boys at Stonyhurst), and with an extraordinary sense of humour, but somehow on a different wave-length. He had no interest in sport – while I still had pretensions as a tennis-player – and scholarship as such did not attract him. Moreover there was a radical toughness about him that I found a little forbidding.

So when we renewed contact as priests, some time in the 1970s, I was pleasantly surprised to find that we had more in common than I had suspected. He was working then with James Walsh on *The Way*, an assignment that I would have found very difficult. He was asked to comment on a contribution I had offered them, and the warmth of his reaction gave me a support that I badly needed. This was to be the pattern of our relationship. Some people have supposed that

I was the one who supported him, but nearly always it was the other way round.

With his illness in the late 1980s it became clear that his commentary on the Exercises would need an editor, and (largely through the efforts of Billy Hewett) I offered to help. Michael agreed and a quite bulky typescript was sent to me at Campion Hall. Fortunately the indefatigable Br James Harkess was willing to scan this for me, so that I could begin editing work on it, using my own Macintosh computer.

There came a stage when Billy and I saw that Michael's revisions and additions would never end, but we were lucky enough to hit on a simple plan (I suspect even Michael later saw that it was something of a ruse): we persuaded him to channel all his additions into what would be a second volume, which even had a title, *Ignatian Words*, and was to be an extended glossary. Michael continued working on this after the publication of *Understanding the Spiritual Exercises* (in 1998), but as his ambitions for the second volume grew, and his energies diminished, I could see that it would never see the light of day. In addition, a similar project had been launched in Spain, organized by an enthusiastic group of young Jesuits. They asked Michael to contribute, but as far as I know he was not able to complete anything.

All of this activity meant that I established a new relationship with Michael, much helped by the quiet encouragement of Mary Reidy. The toughness that I had seen earlier, and which had rather intimidated me, now proved to be a rock of good sense and extraordinary optimism. He seemed scared of nothing, and quite oblivious of his own aches and pains – while also very sensitive to the nuances and needs of others. His intelligence remained undiminished, quick, lucid, attentive to the smallest detail and retentive of all one had said. Nothing seemed to shock him. Human nature was like an open book for him: he was a realist, capable of seeing the ridiculous and the pretentious, but also the strong and the good. Other gifts also gradually came to light: his drawings, his appreciation for beautiful things. Even if he did not complain about it, one of the hardships that most pained him was to see his own body, once so slim, become bloated and ungainly. Fortunately there were compensations, like the arrival of his beautiful black Labrador, Lennie, and he was proud to be able to manage his 'talking' computer, and keep up communication by e-mail.

Like so many others, I feel very privileged to have known Michael, and am very grateful to Mary, the good angel who adopted him and kept him alive for so many and such fruitful years. May we all meet merrily one day!

Patrick Purnell, SJ [friend and poet]

The Unraveller
(In memoriam M.I.)

Gifted was he with empathy,
Insight and intuition,
Rooted in a wisdom drawn from a well
Deep within himself;
These were the tools of his trade,
Unravelling the text
His Father Ignatius had penned in a Manresa Cave,
Become now the marrow of his life.
There had always been a waiting,
A waiting on the Spirit
Who came in darkness and in light,
Whose message was discernible
Within the felt patterns
Of a life he slowly yielded
To the One whom he was created
To praise, reverence and serve.
But it was in the closing years,
When darkness made its way
Across the horizons of his eyes,
That God did play his part
In the *Take Lord and Receive*,

And Michael became the poor man in a poverty
Beyond the conceiving thoughts of his imagination,
Readying him to become
That little servant at the crib side,
Tasting the infinite gentleness
And sweetness
Of the Divinity.

Tom Shufflebotham, SJ [Superior of St Beuno's; part of the sermon delivered in the House Chapel on the eve of the funeral]

[He began by outlining the stages of Michael's life] . . .
Meanwhile the book was slowly maturing. It had been
advertised over twenty years earlier, but while Michael
made other contributions to reviews and collections, *the*
book had to await a long gestation. The result in many
people's view, including mine, is that he has given the
world the best unified insight into the Ignatian *Exercises*,
and all expressed in a style that is graceful and lucid and
inspiring. And that reflects the beautiful maturing and
mellowing and enriching of Michael's personality, his
Christian personality, over the years. Possibly in the talk he
gave us long ago as novices on Hopkins there was something a bit flashy and affected. Not so in later years. What
you saw was what you got. Integrity and authenticity
mattered profoundly to Michael.

[Then on Michael's last years and days] . . . During the
last year or two Michael had become unable to walk and
progressively more subject to infections. Sr Mary Reidy
had been caring for him for about fifteen years. Even
though there was an increasing amount of help, thanks to
the excellent local medical practice, Michael's condition
required an ever-greater commitment from Mary, and
without her he would surely not have survived the last few
years; and before that his quality of life would have been
even more diminished. As it was, he continued to converse

with a wide variety of visitors, though in the last few months his awareness and ability to respond was diminished. In recent years Michael had a guide dog, Lennie, whose quiet demeanour and reluctance to bark might suggest that he is permanently on retreat. Lennie, a favourite with everyone, was a great comfort to Michael though 'guiding' became less possible.

In early September yet another infection led to Michael's admission into hospital, but after a couple of days he was comfortable enough to be allowed home. Death was just a matter of time and very limited time at that. He died peacefully on the afternoon of 9 September.

BIBLIOGRAPHY

Works of St Ignatius

Spanish text: *Obras* see *Constitutions*.

Translation: *Saint Ignatius of Loyola: Personal Writings*, translated with introductions and notes by Joseph A. Munitiz and Philip Endean [Penguin Classics], Harmondsworth 1996, 2005[2] [contains *Autobiography (Reminiscences), Spiritual Diary, Letters* (40), *Spiritual Exercises*].

Autobiography (Reminiscences)

See above: *Translation: Personal Writings*

Constitutions

Spanish text: *Obras de San Ignacio de Loyola (Edición Manual)* (eds) Ignacio Iparraguirre, Cándido de Dalmases, Manuel Ruiz Jurado [Biblioteca de Autores Cristianos], Madrid 1991[5].

Translation: *Saint Ignatius of Loyola: The Constitutions of the Society of Jesus*, translated with an Introduction and a Commentary by George E. Ganss, Institute of Jesuit Sources, St Louis 1970 [this text has been reproduced in *The Constitutions of The Society of Jesus and their*

Complementary Norms, Institute of Jesuit Sources, St Louis, 1996].

Letters

Original text published in MHSI, *Monumenta Ignatiana*, Series prima, *Sancti Ignatii de Loyola Epistolae et Instructiones*, Madrid, 1903–14), 12 vols.

Translation: (1) *Inigo: Letters Personal and Spiritual*, selected by Michael Ivens, edited and translated by Joseph A. Munitiz, Inigo Enterprises, 1995 [77 letters].

(2) *Saint Ignatius of Loyola: Personal Writings* [40 letters selected from the above], see Works.

(3) *Letters of St. Ignatius of Loyola*, Selected and translated by William J. Young, Chicago, Loyola University Press, 1959 [228 letters].

(4) Hugo Rahner, *Saint Ignatius Loyola; Letters to Women*, Freiburg, Edinburgh-London, Herder, Nelson, 1960 [tr. *Ignatius von Loyola, Briefwechsel mit Frauen*, Freiburg, Herder, 1956].

(5) Martin E. Palmer, John W. Padberg, John L. McCarthy (eds), *Ignatius of Loyola: Letters and Instructions*, St Louis, Institute of Jesuit Sources, 2006.

Spiritual Diary

See *Saint Ignatius of Loyola: Personal Writings*.

Spiritual Exercises

Spanish text: (1) *Ejercicios espirituales, Directorio y Documentos de S. Ignacio de Loyola*, edited with glossary, José Calveras, Barcelona, 1958[2]. [Concordances, cf. Echarte, I.; Teinonen, S.A].

(2) *Obras de San Ignacio de Loyola* [see above under *Constitutions*].

Translation: (1) *The Spiritual Exercises of Saint Ignatius of Loyola*, translated by Michael Ivens, introduced by

Gerard W. Hughes, Gracewing, Leominster, 2004 [text also available in the commentary: *Understanding the Spiritual Exercises*, see Secondary Literature, s.v. Ivens, Michael.

(2) See *Saint Ignatius of Loyola: Personal Writings*. Vulgate (the name given to the Latin translation of the Exercises presented for approval to Paul III); French translation, *Saint Ignace de Loyola, Exercices spirituals, Texte definitive (1548)*, trans. and commentary by Jean-Claude Guy, Paris, Seuil, 1982.

Secondary Sources

Aelred of Rievaulx, St, *The Mirror of Charity: The Speculum Caritatis*, translated by Geoffrey Webb and Adrian Walker, London, Mowbray, 1962.

Bonhoeffer, Dietrich, *Letters & Papers from Prison*, London, Collins, Fontana, 1953.

Egan, Harvey D., *The Spiritual Exercises and the Ignatian Mystical Horizon* [Series IV, Study Aids on Jesuit Topics, Nr. 5], St Louis, Institute of Jesuit Sources, 1976.

Echarte, Ignacio (ed.), *Concordancia Ignaciana: an Ignatian Concordance*, Bilbao and Maliaño, Mensajero and Sal Terrae, 1996.

de Guibert, Joseph, *The Jesuits: their spiritual doctrine and practice: a historical study* [original French version: *La spiritualité de la compagnie de Jésus: esquisse historique*, Institutum Historicum Societatis Iesu, Rome, 1953], Chicago, Institute of Jesuit Sources, 1964.

Gonçalves da Câmara, Luis, *Memoriale* [tr. Alexander Eaglestone, Joseph A. Munitiz, SJ, *Remembering Iñigo: Glimpses of the Life of Saint Ignatius of Loyola*, Leominster and St Louis, Gracewing and Institute of Jesuit Sources, 2004.]

Hopkins, Gerard Manley, *Poems and Prose of Gerard Manley Hopkins*, (ed.) W. H. Gardner, Harmondsworth, Penguin Books, 1953.

Guigo II, *Letter on the Interior Life* [= *Scala claustralium*], tr. Edmund Colledge and James Walsh, *The Way* 1965, pp. 333–42.

Ivens, Michael, *Understanding the Spiritual Exercises*, Leominster, Gracewing, 1998.

Ivens, Michael [other publications listed above: cf. Part IV, §1.]

Lonsdale, David, *Eyes to See, Ears to Hear; An Introduction to Ignatian Spirituality*, London, Darton Longman & Todd, 1990.

McIntosh, Mark. A., *Mystical Theology: The Integrity of Spirituality and Theology* [Challenges in Contemporary Theology], Oxford, Blackwell, 1998.

Melloni, Javier, *The Exercises of St Ignatius Loyola in the Western Tradition*, Leominster, 2000.

O'Reilly, Terence, 'El tránsito del temor servil al temor filial en los "Ejercicios Espirituales"', (ed.) Juan Plazaola, *Las Fuentes de los Ejercicios Espirituales de San Ignacio*, Bilbao, 1998, pp. 223–41.

Palmer, Martin E. (translator and editor), *On Giving the Spiritual Exercises: the Early Jesuit Manuscript Directories and the Official Directory of 1599*, St Louis, Institute of Jesuit Sources, 1996.

Rahner, Karl, *Spiritual Exercises*, London: Sheed & Ward, 1976 [German edn., 1966].

Teinonen, Seppo A., *Concordancias de los Ejercicios Espirituales de San Ignacio de Loyola* [Annales Academiae Scientiarum Fennicae: Ser. B, t. 211], Helsinki, 1981.

Tanner, SJ, Norman, *Decrees of the Ecumenical Councils*, London and Washington, 1990.

Toner, Jules, *Discerning God's Will: Ignatius of Loyola's Teaching on Christian Decision Making* [Series III: Original Studies Composed in English, Number 8], St Louis, Institute of Jesuit Sources, 1991

Vatican II cf. Tanner, Norman.

INDEX OF SPIRITUAL EXERCISES

[paragraph numbers in square brackets]

INDEX OF SUBJECTS

['cf. Exx.' is added when a subject is found in the previous Index.]

marriage xi, 25–26, 46, 51–52,
    60
Mary xi, 27–31, 69, 99, 136;
    mediator 29–31; titles
    28–29
material subjecta xi [never
    written]
maturity 79, 84, 86, 165
McIntosh, Mark A. 57
mediation xi [never written]; cf.
    Mary
meditation xi, 35, 67–68, 77,
    82
Melloni, Javier 68
memory 110, 117
mendicancy xi
mercy xi [never written]
method of prayer cf. prayer
modern difficulties 102; cf.
    psychology; today
Montserrat 27, 68
Mora, Alfonso de la 124
mortal sin xi, 158
movement of the soul xi
mysticism xi, 32–36

Nadal, Jerome 22
novices 5, 15, 73, 141

only 4, 156
O'Reilly, Terence 128
Ortiz, Dr (retreat notes) 129
Our Lady cf. Mary

Palestine 24
Paschal mystery xi, 15, 33–34,
    116
Paul III 22
Pedroche, Tomás de 22
Pelagianism 120
penance 11
perfection 6, 19, 39, 46, 120
petition xi, 23, 27, 69, 77–78,

83–86, 89, 90, 113
points 77, 90
Polanco, Juan 22, 73
polyphony 157
Pousset, Edouard 65
poverty xi, 6, 15, 24, 25, 27,
    33, 36–41, 42, 63, 64, 65,
    83, 102, 113, 122, 123;
    spiritual/actual 37–39, 80.
    115–116, 161; 'state' 39–40
powers of the soul xi [never
    written]
prayer xi, 10, 16, 22, 27, 32, 35,
    46, 48, 54, 63, 72, 78, 82,
    86–91, 92, 121, 141, 143,
    163; methods xi, 77, 88–91;
    cf. colloquy; contemplation;
    examen; Exx.; history; imag-
    ination; *lectio divina*;
    meditation; petition
preludes 90
pride xi, 38, 64, 70, 113;
    159–160
profit xi, 161–162
psychology 37, 45, 57, 86,
    104, 106, 117, 131, 134;
    cf. intention; self

Rahner, Hugo 26
Rahner, Karl 126, 130
reading 68
reason cf. imagination
recreation 92
Reformation 9
Rejadell, Teresa 153
religious life xi, 42–43, 46, 60,
    148
*Reminiscences cf. Autobiog-
    raphy*
repentance 158
repetition 14
repose days xi, 91–93
reverence xi, 10, 16, 20, 95,

Printed in the United States
144965LV00004B/41/A